Editor-in-Chief and Founder:
  Lyndon H. LaRouche, Jr.
Editorial Board: *Lyndon H. LaRouche, Jr. , Helga
  Zepp-LaRouche, Robert Ingraham, Tony
  Papert, Gerald Rose, Dennis Small, Jeffrey
  Steinberg, William Wertz*
Co-Editors: *Robert Ingraham, Tony Papert*
Managing Editor: *Nancy Spannaus*
Technology: *Marsha Freeman*
Books: *Katherine Notley*
Ebooks: *Richard Burden*
Graphics: *Alan Yue*
Photos: *Stuart Lewis*
Circulation Manager: *Stanley Ezrol*

INTELLIGENCE DIRECTORS
Counterintelligence: *Jeffrey Steinberg, Michele
  Steinberg*
Economics: *John Hoefle, Marcia Merry Baker,
  Paul Gallagher*
History: *Anton Chaitkin*
Ibero-America: *Dennis Small*
Russia and Eastern Europe: *Rachel Douglas*
United States: *Debra Freeman*

INTERNATIONAL BUREAUS
Bogotá: *Miriam Redondo*
Berlin: *Rainer Apel*
Copenhagen: *Tom Gillesberg*
Houston: *Harley Schlanger*
Lima: *Sara Madueño*
Melbourne: *Robert Barwick*
Mexico City: *Gerardo Castilleja Chávez*
New Delhi: *Ramtanu Maitra*
Paris: *Christine Bierre*
Stockholm: *Ulf Sandmark*
United Nations, N.Y.C.: *Leni Rubinstein*
Washington, D.C.: *William Jones*
Wiesbaden: *Göran Haglund*

ON THE WEB
e-mail: eirns@larouchepub.com
www.larouchepub.com
www.executiveintelligencereview.com
www.larouchepub.com/eiw
Webmaster: *John Sigerson*
Assistant Webmaster: *George Hollis*
Editor, Arabic-language edition: *Hussein Askary*

EIR (ISSN 0273-6314) *is published weekly
(50 issues), by EIR News Service, Inc.,
P.O. Box 17390, Washington, D.C. 20041-0390.
(703) 777-9451 ext. 415*

European Headquarters: E.I.R. GmbH, Postfach
Bahnstrasse 9a, D-65205, Wiesbaden, Germany
Tel: 49-611-73650
Homepage: http://www.eirna.com
e-mail: eirna@eirna.com
Director: Georg Neudecker

Montreal, Canada: 514-461-1557

Denmark: EIR - Danmark, Sankt Knuds Vej 11,
basement left, DK-1903 Frederiksberg, Denmark.
Tel.: +45 35 43 60 40, Fax: +45 35 43 87 57. e-mail:
eirdk@hotmail.com.

Mexico City: EIR, Sor Juana Inés de la Cruz 242-2
Col. Agricultura C.P. 11360
Delegación M. Hidalgo, México D.F.
Tel. (5525) 5318-2301
eirmexico@gmail.com

Canada Post Publication Sales Agreement
#40683579

Postmaster: Send all address changes to *EIR*, P.O.
Box 17390, Washington, D.C. 20041-0390.

Signed articles in *EIR* represent the views of the
authors, and not necessarily those of the Editorial
Board.

Crush the
British Empire

EDITORIAL

THE TIME IS NOW

Crush the British Empire Once and For All!

Jan. 24—Many have doubted the warning of Lyndon LaRouche, over these past 50 years, that the British Empire is still alive, and still dedicated to crushing the American System of Alexander Hamilton, John Quincy Adams, Abraham Lincoln, and Franklin Roosevelt. But today those doubts have been proven to be most foolish, as the imperial lords of the City of London and the British Monarchy have declared themselves, proudly, to be intent on destroying any effort to restore the American System in the United States, their former colonies.

The Obama years proved to be the total takeover of the U.S. government by the British System. The "free trade" model of the British, which America's Founding Fathers had fought a revolution to escape, succeeded in eliminating all of the Frankin Roosevelt regulations and restraints on Wall Street, creating a speculative bubble reaching into the mega-trillions.

The British opium war on China was superseded in evil by the British and Wall Street banks' "Dope, Inc.," creating the worst drug epidemic in U.S. history, while Obama refused to jail the bankers responsible for either the financial crash or the drug money laundering, and openly promoted drug legalization. Industry was dismantled under the guise of both "free trade" and the hoax that carbon was destroying the planet, all sponsored by Prince Philip's World Wildlife Fund and related green fanatics. Space exploration and the scientific development of nuclear and fusion power were destroyed under the same British imperial model of enforced backwardness.

Perpetual, colonial wars have been waged against nations that were no threat to the United States, but were too close to Russia or China, using the British/Saudi-funded terror networks to remove governments by force. Obama and his British sponsors prepared for war with Russia and China with a massive military encirclement of both Eurasian nations.

Revive the Spirit of the War of Independence

The threat to this British control over the United States, represented by the defeat of the Obama/Hillary evil in November, has now forced the British out into the open, willing to kill to stop any chance that the Trump Administration might restore sanity. They must be stopped, and the British System destroyed, if civilization is to survive this crisis.

Look at three developments of the past months:

• It is now known that the entire, hysterical campaign to portray Donald Trump as a Russian tool was run by "former" MI6 agent Christopher Steele, who fabricated a document so absurd that even the British assets in the U.S. intelligence community had to admit that they could not confirm any of it, despite the fact that they themselves had leaked it to the public.

• The *London Spectator* published an article by BBC journalist Paul Wood on Jan. 21, titled, "Will Donald Trump Be Assassinated, Ousted in a Coup or Just Impeached?" Remember that the British have a tradition of assassinating American presidents who have stood up against the Empire—Lincoln, Garfield, McKinley, and Kennedy.

• A legal case has been introduced in New York accusing President Trump of breaching the Constitution by owning hotels that occasionally accept foreign govenment officials as guests—this supposedly constituting bribes and payoffs to the President. The case is being brought by "Citizens for Responsibility and Ethics in Washington," a group funded by the notorious British asset George Soros, the world's leading public promoter of drug legalization, euthanasia, color revolutions, and operations against the Russian and Chinese governments.

Despite the Soros campaign against President Trump, whom he labeled a "would-be dictator," an associate of Soros, Steven Mnuchin, has been chosen as Trump's Treasury Secretary. Mnuchin worked in two hedge funds heavily funded by Soros, and worked directly for Soros Fund Management at one point. Mnuchin, in his confirmation hearing, flatly stated that he and Trump would not support the restoration of Glass-Steagall, despite the fact that Trump had pledged to restore Glass-Steagall during the campaign. The British Foreign Office in 2012 informed an American economist visiting the City of London, that passage of the Glass-Steagall legislation, then before the Congress due primarily to extensive organizing by LaRouche PAC, was a *casus belli*, a justification for war.

That war is now engaged. That the new American Administration will reject the British System—in favor of Glass-Steagall, of cooperation with Russia in combatting terrorism rather than overthrowing sovereign governments, and of joining with China in the New Silk Road development of the entire world—is not certain, but is definitely possible. What is required is the mobilization of the American people to acknowledge the evil of the British System and to crush it, protecting President Trump and the nation from the assault on humanity now in play from a desperate British Empire. The time is now.

We must mobilize the American people to revive the spirit of the War of Independence against the British Empire, of Lincoln's defense of the Union, and of FDR's fight against Wall Street. It can be done, but we need to bring to life all of the best traditions of American history. We need you.

EIR Contents

www.larouchepub.com Volume 44, Number 4, January 27, 2017

Cover This Week

I. The New Paradigm

KRA CANAL CLOSE TO A REALITY

A Hub for the Maritime Silk Road

by Michael Billington

Jan. 21—The concept of cutting a canal through the Isthmus of Kra in southern Thailand, has been a conception in the minds of visionary thinkers for hundreds of years. In the early 1980s, it nearly came to fruition, as associates of Lyndon LaRouche—including especially Pakdee Tanapura of Thailand—mobilized leaders of the Thai government, American scientific institutions, Japan's Mitsubishi Global Infrastructure Fund (GIF), and leaders from every major country in the region (except Singapore and China), to two conferences in Bangkok dedicated to implementing this great project to unite the Pacific and Indian Ocean Basins via a canal.

But the British Empire has repeatedly, throughout history, acted to stop the building of the Kra Canal for two reasons: Because they wanted to maintain the strategic chokehold over Asian trade which they enjoyed through their colonial outpost in Singapore and the Malacca Strait, but primarily because such a project would facilitate cooperation among the Asian nations for mutual development, and resistance to western imperial dictate—a result to be feared and undermined by the Empire.

Financial and political crises in the 1990s, caused by British financial interests and their lackeys such as George Soros, prevented the implementation of the Kra Canal project during the final decades of the 20th Century and the early 21st Century. But now the world is experiencing a global revolutionary transformation, and the British Empire, including its puppet Bush and Obama regimes in Washington, is facing dissolution. A new paradigm has emerged, centered in China, bringing Russia, India, Southeast Asia, and potentially the entire world into its development orientation, the "win-win" perspective of Chinese President Xi Jinping's New Silk Road perspective, known as the Belt and Road Initiative (BRI).

EIRNS

Lyndon LaRouche responding to a question from the floor on Oct. 27, 1983 at the Development of the Pacific and Indian Ocean Basins conference in Bangkok, Thailand. Pakdee Tanapura is seated on the right.

FIGURE 1

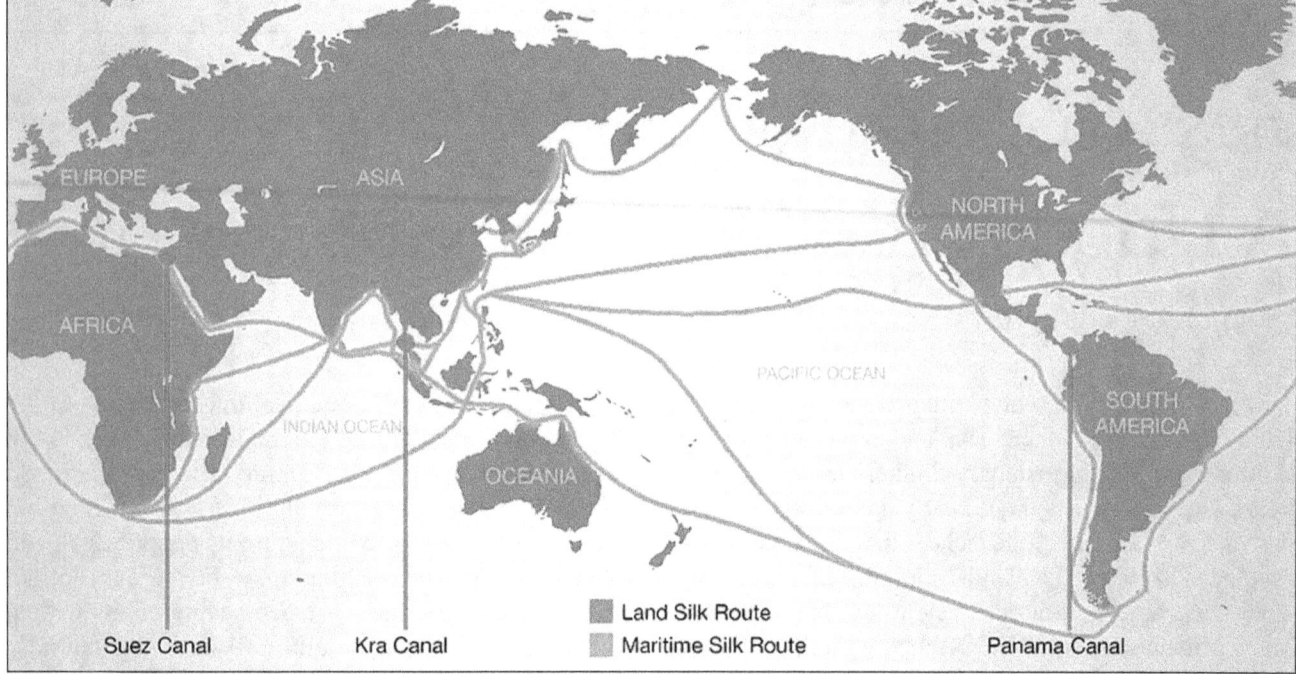

| Suez Canal | Kra Canal | ■ Land Silk Route | Panama Canal |
| | | ■ Maritime Silk Route | |

In South and Southeast Asia, China's "21st Century Maritime Silk Road" concept (see **Figure 1**), introduced by President Xi in 2013 while speaking to the Indonesian Parliament, has already brought the nations along the South China Sea, the Malacca Strait, the Andaman Sea, the Bay of Bengal, the Indian Ocean, the Arabian Sea, and through the Suez Canal to the Mediterranean, into an entirely new economic and political geometry based on rapid infrastructure development.

But missing from this geometry has been the hub represented by the potential of the Kra Canal. Now that potential is very close to realization, as the entire Asian region is breaking away from British/American constraints, and acting in its own interests to facilitate "win-win" development for all parties. At the same time, leading political forces in Thailand are now in a position to launch the project.

Strategic Heritage of Thailand

This week, a book has been released in Thailand, in the Thai language, titled in English *Kra Canal: Strategic Heritage of Thailand*, published by the Lexnova Consultant Company Limited in Bangkok. *EIR*'s associate in Thailand, Pakdee Tanapura, a Member of the Board of Directors and the International Director of the International Executive Committee for the Study of the Kra Canal Project, is one of its principal authors. Also contributing to the book are:

•General Thawatchai Samutsakorn, a Member of the National Reform Council, a government advisory body which has prepared policy proposals for the interim government under former General Prayut Chanocha, and is preparing a new Constitution for the nation;

•General Pradit Boonkerd, a Board Member of General Prem Tinsulanonda's Foundation (General Prem is Chairman of the Privy Council);

•Admiral Suphakorn Kunnadilok, former Commander of the Royal Thai Navy's fleets;

•Dr. Surin Dulwatanachit, deputy chairman of the Thai-Chinese Cultural and Economic Association.

This very high-powered group has come together at a propitious moment. First, there is a new King in Thailand, as Crown Prince Vajiralongkorn officially took the throne on Dec. 1 following the death in October of his father, King Bhumibol, who had been King for 70 years. Several leading members of the new Privy Council for King Vajiralongkorn, including its President, Prem Tinsulanonda, are promoting the Kra Canal project, and all indications are that the King is also in favor.

FIGURE 2

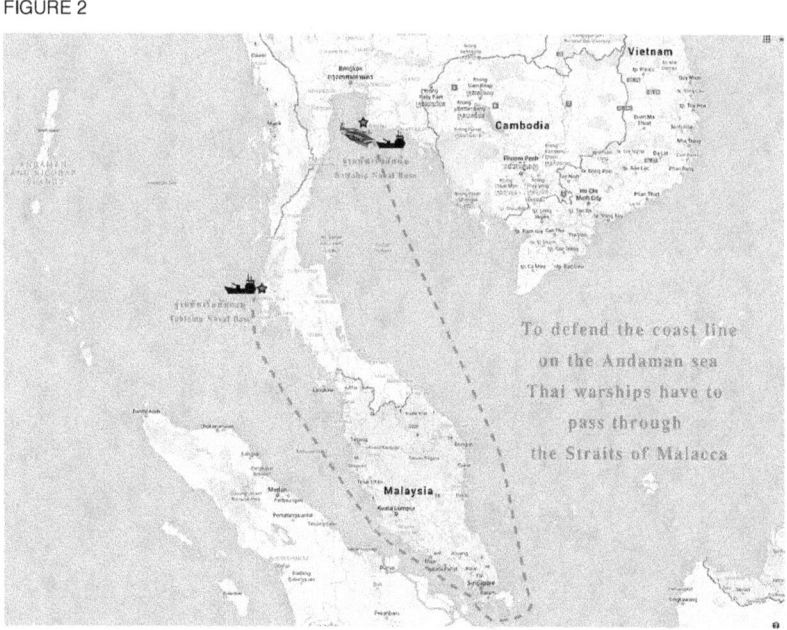

kracanal-maritimesilkroad.com

The Thai Navy must pass through the Singapore choke point of the Malacca Strait to defend its coastline on the Andaman Sea.

Although the interim government of Prime Minister Prayut has indicated that it will not proceed with the Canal project during his term in office, the Royal support could change that perspective. In any case, an election is expected next year.

The first printing of the new book on the Kra Canal produced 10,000 copies, and already 6,500 have been purchased, of which 5,000 are being distributed to leading institutions and individuals around the country.

Even more important for the future of the Kra Canal, the British/American imperial policy of dividing Asia into blocs—based on a group of American allies (primarily the Philippines, Japan, South Korea, and Australia)—which served the Obama policy of encircling China militarily and economically, is crumbling in the face of China's Silk Road development policies. The Philippines, under its new President Rodrigo Duterte, has completely rejected any idea of participation in a military confrontation with China, and is calling on China and Russia to help restore the decaying Philippine economy and to aid in its war on drugs. Japan's Prime Minister Shinzo Abe has joined with Russia's President Vladimir Putin in a massive joint development perspective for the Russian Far East, while setting a course for resolving territorial issues left over from World War II. And South Korea's President Park Geun-hye, who deserted her original Eurasia Initiative in favor of Obama's demand to deploy THAAD missiles in her country—a direct provocation against China and Russia—is now under impeachment and likely to be removed from office.

And, over the past few years, Thailand, once the primary military base for America's bloody and self-destructive war in Indochina, has come to look to China for the infrastructure development which it never got from the United States. Not only is China building a rail connection from the Laos border to Bangkok and to the major ports southeast of Bangkok, but a Chinese firm has now completed a feasibility study of the Kra Canal.

Benefits

The website www.kracanal-maritime-silkroad.com/en/, run by the Thai-Chinese Cultural and Economic Association, presents the extensive benefits the Kra Canal will provide to the world. For Thailand itself, the southern provinces are the poorest in the nation, and are plagued by a terrorist threat fed by Saudi Wahhabi networks among the Muslim population there (See **Figure 2**). The Canal, and the ports and industrial parks at either end of it, will provide jobs and prosperity for the area, helping to unite the nation.

For Asia, the Canal will become the hub for rapidly expanding trade and cooperation between India and China, between Japan and Korea, and between Africa and Southwest Asia on the one side, and with all of East Asia on the other. For the world as a whole, the growing centrality of Asian trade and development in the world economy means that the benefits of the Kra Canal will be universal.

International Support

In the 1980s, the primary international support for the Kra Canal project came from Japan's Mitsubishi Global Infrastructure Fund, and that institution is still actively supporting the project. But China has emerged as a great power since that time, and Xi Jinping's "Belt and Road Initiative" is already transforming the world. China has shown considerable interest in the Kra Canal project as a potential hub of the "21st Century Maritime Silk Road."

Daisuke Kotegawa, a former Japanese Ministry of

Finance official and former Japanese Executive Director at the IMF—now at the Canon Institute in Tokyo—is a strong supporter of the project. Mr. Kotegawa points out that the project would be equally beneficial to Japan and China (as well as others), and it would thus be of mutual interest for the two nations to join forces, with Thailand, in funding and building the Canal. This would, at the same time, help build trust between the two giant economies of Asia, towards overcoming the still festering tensions between them as a result of the legacy of war. The Asian Development Bank (ADB), whose President is Japanese and whose Vice-President is Chinese, is already participating in joint projects with the new Asian Infrastructure Investment Bank (AIIB) established under Xi Jinping in China. If Thailand were to call on both banks to participate in funding this project, it would help tremendously in the process of building trust and peace through development, throughout Asia (See **Figure 3**).

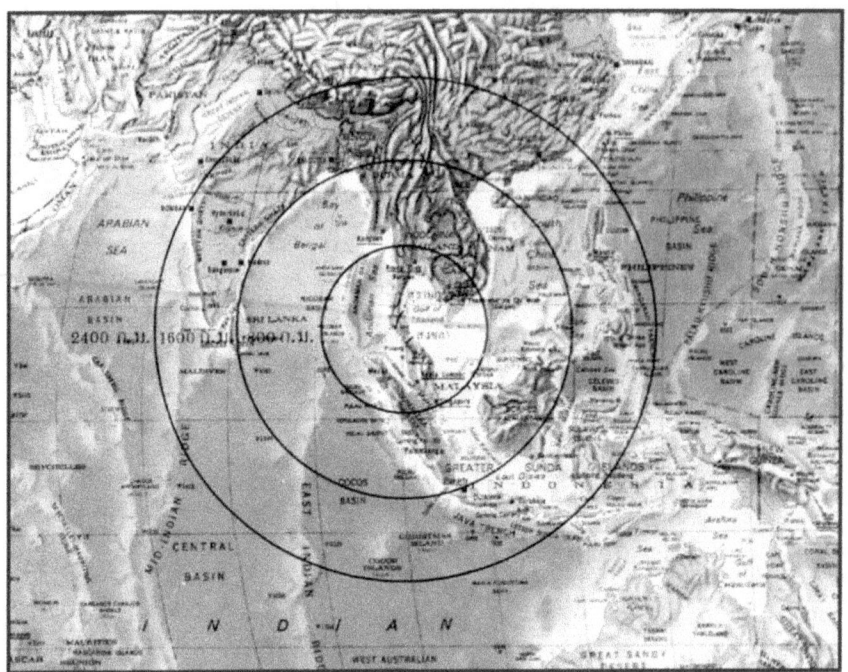

kracanal-maritimesilkroad.com

The Kra Canal as the hub for the Indian and Pacific Ocean basins.

Until now, Washington has played the British role in Asia, offering no encouragement—let alone support—for the Kra Canal, nor for any other major infrastructure projects in Asia. But that may well be about to change. The West is in a process of turmoil and revolution, with no more dramatic change than the defeat of the Barack Obama/Hillary Clinton war policies in the U.S. Presidential election. Under George W. Bush and Obama, the United States had descended into perpetual warfare across Southwest Asia, while carrying out a massive military buildup on both the Russian and Chinese borders. Obama called the provocative buildup against China, his "pivot to Asia."

But President-elect Trump has declared an end to regime change wars, and committed the United States to work with Russia in waging a serious war on terrorism. While he has criticized China on trade issues, he is committed to cooperation with China on business matters, as indicated by his meeting with Alibaba's Jack Ma. Xi Jinping has repeatedly called on the United States to join in the new Silk Road and the AIIB, which Obama flatly rejected, to America's detriment. President Trump has indicated an openness to such cooperation.

The New Paradigm

There is no more important task facing the world today than that of bringing the United States into partnership with Russia and China, both to confront and destroy the terrorist scourge emanating from the British assets in Saudi Arabia, and to cooperate in the New Paradigm of win-win development policies throughout the world, as launched by China under the Belt and Road Initiative.

Lyndon LaRouche, who was the keynote speaker at the Kra Canal conferences in Bangkok in 1983 and 1984, was interviewed in 2014 by *Fortune Times* of Singapore on the Kra Canal. LaRouche said:

Divide the maritime region of East and South Asia into three principal categories: China, a giant; India, a giant; and the maritime connection, throughout Southeast Asia's maritime regions. Add the impact of such triadic maritime and related connections, to the physical-economic relations to the Americas to the East, and the Middle East's underbelly and Africa. Then, the potency of a Kra Canal development appears not only as an eminently feasible feature, but as a strategic political-economic force for the planet.

LaRouche also noted that the primary opposition to the Kra Canal within Asia is Singapore, and that the chief source of resistance from Singapore is entirely global, British-imperial military-strategic interests. But, he added:

The sheer volume of maritime trade between the two great nations of Asia [China and India], and their connections through the South Asia maritime regions, make the Canal probably the most potentially beneficial, and also efficient project for the entire region of the Pacific and Indian Ocean regions, and the co-development of the major regions of Planet Earth as a whole.

As to Singapore, LaRouche added: "Singapore itself, when freed from British strategic imperatives, will benefit far more from the success of the Kra Canal development, than without the development of the Kra!"

In another context, in 2015, LaRouche told his associates:

With the completion of the Kra Canal, on top of the Suez Canal expansion, there will no longer be a separation between the Atlantic and the Pacific economies. China and India will greatly benefit from these two canal projects, along with the smaller nations along the Southeast Asian rim. This must be pushed hard! This will end the British geopolitical games in the Eurasian region. It will change the economic character of the entire world. Australia will be hard-pressed to stay out of this enterprise, and the Australian participation will further erode the British maritime choke-point games that have stymied the true prospects for economic integration and vast increases in trade and development.

A 41-minute video on the Kra Canal, produced in 2013 by the LaRouche Political Action Committee, can be viewed at LPAC.co/KraCanal. The video has had over 23,000 views since its release.

Chinese President at Davos Calls For Reform of Global Governance

by William Jones

Jan. 22—While a great deal of attention has been focused this past week on the inauguration of the new U.S. president, Donald Trump, perhaps the most important event that actually occurred was at the World Economic Forum at Davos, where President Xi Jinping gave two extremely important speeches regarding the present world economic crisis.

While President Xi, in his speeches, emphasized his theme that the world has to become a "community of a shared future," the media tried to portray the Chinese President as simply a promoter of "globalization," as this concept has generally been understood prior to the launch of the Belt and Road policy. What the media failed to realize is that what President Xi was presenting was indeed something quite new and exciting.

While President Xi spoke warmly about the importance of "economic globalization," he was not characterizing that system by which "supranational institutions" have subordinated entire nations to their dictate, by eliminating, in many cases, the power of the sovereign governments to determine their own policy. Nor was his concept of "economic globalization" a defense of that system in which the uncontrolled movement of finance capital from country to country and region to region could proceed unimpeded, in its unending search for maximum profit, often at the cost of the lives, the well-being, and the health of their "host countries."

The world-wide reaction to "globalization" has been a reaction against this type of system. The concept of "economic globalization" that President Xi was calling for in his "community of a shared future," is actually a unique vision that is inclusive, cooperative, and compassionate. We might even designate it "globalization with Chinese characteristics."

World Economic Forum/Manuel Lopez

People's Republic of China President Xi Jinping, speaking at the World Economic Forum in Davos, Switzerland, Jan. 17, 2017.

To American opponents of the destructive, lunatic, British-imperial policies of Obama, Bush, and Cheney, President Xi's "globalization with Chinese characteristics" is so utterly different from what they have known as "globalization" under these past U.S. administrations, that it seems to be its direct opposite.

For the Chinese President, "economic globalization" is the process by which world civilization has developed through the ages, gradually creating that worldwide division of labor which now forms the basis for the conditions of life of every individual today.

"From the historical perspective," Xi said, "economic globalization resulted from growing social productivity, and is a natural outcome of scientific and technological progress, not something created by any individuals or any countries. Economic globalization has powered global growth and facilitated movement of goods and capital, advances in science, technology, and civilization, and interactions among peoples."

At the same time, he clearly indicated that the world can no longer accept certain aspects that have accompanied this development: "But we should also recognize that economic globalization is a double-edged sword," President Xi said. "When the global economy is under downward pressure, it is hard to make the 'cake' of the global economy bigger. It may even shrink, which will strain the relations between growth and distribution, between capital and labor, and between efficiency and equity. Both developed and developing countries have felt the pinch. Voices against globalization have laid bare the pitfalls in the process of economic globalization that we need to take seriously."

More importantly, President Xi pointed to one of the major problems facing the economic system today: the untrammeled "right" of finance capital to pursue *its* interests in an uncontrolled manner, leading to the major financial crisis in 2008. "The international financial crisis is another example," Xi said. "It is not an inevitable outcome of economic globalization; rather, it is the consequence of the excessive chasing of profit by financial capital and the grave failure of financial regulation."

The key concept in President Xi's understanding of "economic globalization" is development. "Development is ultimately for the people. To achieve more balanced development and ensure that the people have equal access to opportunities and share in the benefits of development, it is crucial to have a sound development philosophy and model, and make development equitable, effective, and balanced," Xi said.

President Xi also underlined the fact that each nation has the right to choose its own path of development, and not have one imposed upon it from the outside. "Sovereign equality is the most important norm governing state-to-state relations over the past centuries, and is the cardinal principle observed by the United Nations and all other international organizations. The essence of sovereign equality is that the sovereignty and dignity of all countries, whether big or small, strong or weak, rich or poor, must be respected, allowing no interference in their internal affairs, and they have the right to independently choose their social system and development path."

The Westphalian Principle

In his speech, Xi made reference to the Peace of Westphalia, which has become a template for later international conventions, including the Geneva Convention, the UN Charter, and the Five Principles of Peaceful Coexistence adopted by Third World Nations at the Bandung conference in 1955. The Treaty of Westphalia had resolved the religious wars in Europe, wars which merged into a single, devastating Thirty Years' War on the European continent. It is grounded on the concept of the "good of the other." As the treaty clearly states: "And this peace and amity shall be observed and cultivated with such a sincerity and zeal, that each party shall endeavor to procure the benefit, honor, and advantage of the other."

American statesman Lyndon H. LaRouche, Jr., gave a perfectly precise statement of the 21st-century version of the Westphalian system in a private discussion with associates on Jan. 21. "What we want, clearly, is security for governments, and the rights of governments to negotiate their own proposed plan of actions," he said. No one can possibly know all the issues and all their solutions in advance, Mr. LaRouche indicated. "Therefore, you've got to open the gates, because you're creating a new system, a system which has not existed as such heretofore, and therefore the gates have to be opened to allow this question to be laid out. That every nation has a right to make a proposal towards the contract among the nations. And the point is, that if you get into that thing, you may get into an argument—but you can solve the argument by finding a solution."

Four decades of Russia-China negotiations, which took those two nations all the way from armed border conflicts in 1969, to an unparalleled, still-deepening strategic alliance today, illustrate these principles outlined by Mr. LaRouche.

While nations, in working together to resolve the problems facing mankind, will inevitably have differences over policy—whether it be a question of territorial disputes, trade disputes, or other matters—such issues can only be settled through negotiations in an attempt to achieve a mutually beneficial result, which the Chinese call a "win-win" situation.

While China and the United States, with the new

orientation of the Trump Administration, will no doubt both be making adjustments in their trade arrangements, the media speculation about a trade war between the United States and China is highly exaggerated. The economic ties between these two great nations and their importance in the world economy does require, as the Chinese President has said, the creation of a "new relationship between major powers."

And as President Xi emphasized in his Davos comments, "There are no winners in a trade war." If President Trump is sincere in following through on his promises to rebuild the U.S. economy, building infrastructure and creating jobs, China could well become his most important ally. Chinese investment in the United States has already created, according to the Rhodium Group's estimate, over 27,000 jobs.

RT.jpg

Chinese businessman Jack Ma (right), met then President-elect Donald Trump Jan. 9, prior to Ma's appearance Jan. 18 at the World Economic Forum. Ma stated at the Forum that the United States wasted $14 trillion over the last 30 years by overly focusing on war and Wall Street, instead of building the economy.

Jack Ma, the CEO of Alibaba, indicated in his discussion with Trump, that creating a new e-link to Chinese consumers for American products, could lead to the employment by U.S. firms of one million more workers here. Chinese expertise in infrastructure development, in particular in high-speed rail, could be of great assistance in revamping our failing transportation grid, putting U.S. workers back to work, building a modern railroad system. While all elements of Hamiltonian economics—tariffs, taxes, and credit issuance—will no doubt also be on the table, there is no reason that the United States and China can't come to a win-win agreement. And U.S. industry, which still maintains a highly qualified labor force, can produce high-quality products that can be of use to China in its own development.

And both countries have a clear interest in getting control over an international financial system which for so long has been totally out of control, resulting in more than one major financial crisis in the last twenty years. Governments must decide their own national policies, and not the board of directors at some mega-investment bank. A new form of global governance is indeed on the agenda. President Trump has promised Glass-Steagall reform here in the United States, in order to protect the savings, the pensions, and the very existence of U.S. citizens from the depredations of the Wall Street speculators. The same must be done internationally as well.

As President Xi said in his speech at Davos: "The global financial market needs to be more resilient against risks, but the global financial governance mechanism fails to meet the new requirement, and is thus unable to effectively resolve problems such as frequent international financial market volatility and the build-up of asset bubbles. As the Chinese saying goes," Xi continued, "people with petty shrewdness attend to trivial matters, while people with vision attend to governance of institutions. There is a growing call from the international community for reforming the global economic governance system, which is a pressing task for us. Only when it adapts to new dynamics in the international economic architecture, can the global governance system sustain global growth."

It seems that the crying need for a "new international economic architecture" which will benefit all the countries of the world, could well be the focus around which these two major countries can form a new relationship, in order to see that such an architecture becomes a reality for all mankind. And it will require "vision" from both countries' leaders to bring this to fruition.

America First, or a Common Destiny For the Future of Mankind?

by Helga Zepp-LaRouche, chairwoman of the German political party Civil Rights Movement Solidarity (BüSo)

Jan. 21—President Donald Trump's inaugural address contained a mixture of interesting promises, reminiscences of earlier periods of American history, impractical proclamations, and what is unfortunately the all-too-common notion in the United States—that there is no real world beyond the American continent, which he expressed in the slogan "America First!" It will become apparent over the next days and weeks how he intends to implement his pledge to massively boost the economy, and how foreign relations, especially with Russia and China, will take shape.

C-Span screen capture

President Donald Trump delivers his inaugural address, Jan. 20, 2017.

Russian Prime Minister Dimitry Medvedev commented Jan. 19 that Obama's biggest foreign policy mistake was to have brought relations with Russia down to zero, and that his "reckless" policy of interference in the internal affairs of other countries, such as Iraq, Ukraine, and Syria, had cost thousands of human lives.[1] If Trump abides by his promises, he will correct this error. While the Obama Administration rejected Russia's invitation to participate in the Syrian peace talks in Astana, Kazakhstan, Trump's team has signaled its willingness to take part in this process, which began Jan. 23.

On the same day that Trump took office, Russian Foreign Minister Sergei Lavrov, speaking at a ministerial meeting of the Shanghai Cooperation Organization, stressed the absolute necessity of creating a truly universal anti-terror coalition, as proposed by President Putin at the UN General Assembly in 2015. The unprecedented increase in terrorist activity is the greatest threat to global security, he said. In this fight a great deal depends upon the West, but especially the U.S. administration. For his part, Trump emphasized his intent to go after radical Islamic terror—an intention which is evident in his choices of many cabinet members and advisors.

If you look at the European commentaries on Trump's inaugural address, it is obvious that many representatives of the mainstream media—and many poli-

---

1. https://www.rt.com/news/374268-obama-mistake-relations-russia/

ticians—consider the enemy to be not ISIS, but Trump. German journalist Roland Nelles, for example, is typical of the Fourth Estate, which uses the instruments of NATO's black propaganda to depict snow as black and to blame the sufferings of the peoples of Southwest Asia *not* on Zbigniew Brzezinski's "Islamic card" against (originally) the Soviet Union, but on Putin and Russia. This caste of court scribblers will lose influence if Russian-American cooperation creates facts on the ground that such post-truth commentators cannot account for.

C-Span screen capture

Sen. Maria Cantwell questions Treasury Secretary nominee Steven Mnuchin on Glass-Steagall, Jan. 19, 2017.

The Economic Challenge

Trump's commitment to "build new roads and highways and bridges and airports and tunnels and railways all across our wonderful nation," can bring about a real reversal of the U.S. economic decline. But the absolutely crucial issue is whether he will honor his electoral promise to re-enact Glass-Steagall, made on October 26, 2016, in Charlotte, North Carolina,[2] and thus end the casino economy.

However, the testimony of Trump's Treasury Secretary-designate, Steven Mnuchin, who worked for Goldman Sachs until 2002, raised doubts about the meaning of Trump's statement, when questioned by Senator Maria Cantwell (D-WA) during his Jan. 19 confirmation hearing. Mnuchin contended that it would not be possible to return to the original Glass-Steagall law, but rather, a new version is needed, because otherwise there would be too many liquidity problems in the financial markets. His argument reflects the line of the American Enterprise Institute.

Lyndon LaRouche stresses expressly that only the original Glass-Steagall law, as applied by FDR in 1933, could reorganize the hopelessly bankrupt financial system. Of course there would be a lack of liquidity, if the illegitimate debts, derivatives, and toxic paper of all kinds were written off. That is why Glass-Steagall is

only the first step and would absolutely need to be completed by the other three points of LaRouche's "four laws," namely, the creation of a national bank in the tradition of Alexander Hamilton; a credit system to reconstruct the physical economy; and a crash program to develop both fusion energy and international cooperation in space research. That is the only way the urgently needed rise in productivity of the labor force can be achieved.

Therefore the LaRouche Political Action Committee (LaRouche PAC), in collaboration with an array of other organizations, such as Democrats from Ohio and the Americans for Financial Reform, will escalate their mobilization to put on the agenda FDR's Glass-Steagall Act in its original form, as well as LaRouche's "Four Laws" as a comprehensive package.

Trump is of course right when he raises the problems of the deplorable condition of American industry as a consequence of globalization, or the drug plague, criminality, and so forth. The problem with his campaign slogan, "America First," is that the world has long since developed past the point where the defense of even legitimate national interests is adequate.

A Common Destiny for Mankind

The alternative to Anglo-American style globalization—the current system, which favors the international oligarchy at the expense of the general welfare—is not a return to simple national sovereignty. The universal history of mankind has long since reached the point at which only an entirely new paradigm can lead

---

2. https://www.c-span.org/video/?c4630033/trump-glass-steagall

 中国与全球化智库
CENTER FOR CHINA & GLOBALIZATION

Trump's Coming Era:
Challenges, Opportunities and Policy Responses

On Friday, Jan 20th 2017, Donald Trump will officially be sworn in as the 45th president of the United States. As an "outlier" in political science, the President-elect stirred tremendous attention from both within and outside of U.S. with his strong personality and anti-establishment statements. Scholars and politicians believe that under Trump's leadership, major policy changes will be made and might even observe a growing trend of anti-globalization. This report a study of scholars at the Center for China and Globalization

en.ccg.org.cn

The opening of the report on "Trump's Coming Era," released by the Center for China and Globalization on Jan. 19.

the way to the next evolutionary stage. This new paradigm must put the common interests of mankind first; it must proceed from the idea of "one humanity with a common future" as a conception overarching all legitimate national interests; those interests, of course, must never be at odds with the interests of mankind as a whole. This new paradigm must be as distinct from the axiomatics of globalization as the modern era is from the Middle Ages.

Interestingly, Chinese President Xi Jinping had spoken on precisely this subject on Jan. 18 at the United Nations Palace of Nations in Geneva. There he presented his ideas on how to create a "community of a shared future of mankind"; he drew on the long history of international law, from the Peace of Westphalia of 1648, to the Geneva Conventions of 1864-1949, to the Five Principles of peaceful coexistence of the 1955 Bandung Conference, and to the principles of international cooperation today.

Clearly China's initiative for the New Silk Road—the Belt and Road Initiative, in which more than 70 nations are already cooperating—is based precisely on these principles, whose dynamic is developing into win-win cooperation, potentially for the whole world. On January 19, the day before Trump's inauguration, China's Center for China and Globalization held a seminar to launch its report entitled "Trump's Coming Era: Challenges, Opportunities, and Policy Responses," in which it offers cooperation.[3] The report states that cooperation with China is actually necessary if Trump in-

tends to revive the American economy to the extent he has proposed, because there are too many people in the United States who really do not really want the policy shift. American entrepreneurs should not miss out on the great opportunity of cooperation with the nations along the New Silk Road, and the even greater opportunity of cooperating with China itself, it says.

China has tendered the same offer of cooperation to Germany for more than three years now, and many eastern and central European nations, as well as Greece, Portugal, and Switzerland, have already recognized the advantages of cooperation with the New Silk Road.

Perhaps it is an irony of history that it is Trump's election victory that is also leading to this realization in Germany: The Bavarian weekly newspaper, *Bayrische Staatszeitung*, in a Jan. 19 commentary by its editor in chief, proposes that many Europeans' fears of the consequences of Trump's economic policy should lead them to seek major alternative trade arrangements. China is creating a Eurasian economic zone with its New Silk Road, the paper says, in which not only China's billion-strong population, but also the 60 nations collaborating with it, represent an enormous demand for German and Bavarian goods and services. Other opportunities lie in collaborating with China in the emerging African states, according to the newspaper.

The alternative to "America First" lies in the international collaboration of all nations of the world for their common benefit. America urgently needs a New Silk Road which—proceeding from the southern tip of Chile and Argentina, through South and Central America to Alaska, and a tunnel across the Bering Strait—would link the transportation corridors of the two American continents with those of Eurasia. The economic development of the war-devastated Middle East, and of Africa, represents such a weighty challenge for the world as a whole, that the nations of Europe, together with Russia, China, India, Japan, and the United States, must all tackle this mission.

That is the program that the *BüSo* and the Schiller Institute have worked for, for more than a quarter of a century: "The New Silk Road Becomes the World Land-Bridge." There is every reason for optimism that 2017 will be the year when this program is consolidated as the economic basis for the new paradigm.

---

3. The executive summary of the report: http://en.ccg.org.cn/wp-content/uploads/2017/01/Trumps-Coming-Era-Challenges-Opportunities-and-Policy-Responses.pdf

Senator Mike Gravel Speaks on the Incoming Trump Administration

The following is excerpted from an edited transcript of the LaRouche PAC Manhattan Project Dialogue, which took place on January 21, 2017.

Dennis Speed: Hello, my name is Dennis Speed, and on behalf of the LaRouche Political Action Committee, I want to welcome you here today for our first post-Obama dialogue. [applause] We're going to make sure that we don't veer off topic, because of course, there's a lot of that going on right now in the United States. A lot of people are saying things about the Trump speech which they don't really have the right to say. But we do have an assessment and an evaluation from Lyndon LaRouche, both from yesterday and some additional remarks from today. So, I want to first indicate—because many people would not have heard this—what Lyn had to say immediately after the speech; and then follow up with a few remarks about things he said today.

So regarding the inauguration speech, LaRouche said that it was very confused on the surface, and we'll have to see what is behind the surface. On the basis of what had been presented, there wasn't really a clarity on principle there. Helga said that the most important question to consider is, how does Trump deliver on the domestic front on the promises he made; what are the actions he'll concretely take? And on the international side, she pointed out that it's very important for Donald Trump to realize that the world doesn't work the way he indicated in his speech. While there's something important about this slogan "America First!"— and I'll come to that in a moment—the issue is, how do you find common interest shared by many nations, not just "America First." What are the common objectives

Wikimedia Commons

Maurice Robert "Mike" Gravel (born May 13, 1930), is a former Democratic United States Senator from Alaska, having served for two terms, from 1969 to 1981. In 1971 Gravel played a key role in the release of the Pentagon Papers—a large collection of secret government documents pertaining to the Vietnam War—which were made public by former Defense Department analyst Daniel Ellsberg. Gravel inserted 4,100 pages of the Papers into the Congressional Record of his Senate Subcommittee on Buildings and Grounds.
—Wikileaks

of multiple nations, nd how do you act in pursuit of those objectives? What we sometimes also call the common aims of mankind. Lyn also elaborated from there, saying there's no clear principle; it could go in the direction of a unifying principle. But from what's been presented so far, it isn't clear whether that will be exactly the case.

Today, I should say that Lyn made it clear that he was very concerned about the existence of one particular nut in the Trump administration. He was referring to Steven Mnuchin, the Treasury Secretary-designate nominee—and the exchange, in particular, that Mnuchin had with Senator Maria Cantwell on Glass-Steagall. We'll refer more to this, but LaRouche's point was that this guy is a real nut, and this is a real problem. This causes a very dangerous situation, if you allow someone to muddy the waters and be very unclear. Actually, Helga had made some remarks about that as well, saying that it was very good that Cantwell has now made it very clear, that she used her entire time allocation to question him about his intentions on reinstating Glass-Steagall. When the exchange began, when Cantwell asked him simply "Do you support returning to Glass-Steagall?" he replied, "No, I don't support going back to Glass-Steagall as is. I don't support taking a very old law and saying we should adhere to it."

Now of course, Lyn has been extremely clear—as everybody knows—that Roosevelt's Glass-Steagall, as it was, is what has to be reinstated. It is true—and Lyn has made this point, too— that these matters are complicated, but the main point is that this guy Mnuchin is a sophist. You have the problem that we have to have clarity, and that's what we have as a problem as a whole right now in anything we've heard. Lyn also stated that what we have to do is let them clarify their intentions; we don't want to get wrapped up in the commentary which is going on right now. Maybe Trump will reveal what he truly means, but as of now, there is no clear answer. When people think there is an answer, they're wrong; we need to hold back on this. Trump has gotten into things that he has not yet explained, so let him explain them.

We're going to hear from Mike Gravel. I asked Mike to be on, and he wanted to know why. I said, you've seen a lot of administrations; you've seen the good, the bad, the ugly, and the unspeakable. But also, he's done some things on behalf of justice, as people know, about the "Pentagon Papers" and his role with that. Since we don't have Lyndon LaRouche available,

Wikimedia Commons
Donald Trump at his inauguration ceremony.

I wanted to have somebody play the role of the Dutch uncle; meaning, in other words, keeping people honest in refusing to react to the momentary, what's in front of you; the immediate reflex to somehow respond to the latest media assessment of another assessment of another moron who speaks about a process they have no idea about. This we don't want to have; and I thought that in this context, it would be good for him to say a few things and help us in this regard. So, Mike, take it away!

Sen. Mike Gravel: First off, let me associate myself with the remarks that Ben Deniston has just made about the search for a governing principle, and particularly join Lyndon and Helga in their comments and views with respect to the speech at the inaugural by President Trump. The society we live in right now is one where the media is controlled totally by corporate interests, and now you see them jumping around, trying to analyze what Trump means with every word, and so they parse every word that Trump makes; it's a ridiculous situation, truly. Because the inaugural speech was essentially very superficial; and it was typical Trump. When you say well, what does he mean? These are superficial statements, and that's what he means; because his knowledge at this point is very superficial. Just appreciate where he's coming from; here's a real estate developer who's used to dealing in land development; that is, building buildings and golf courses and hotels. Now, that's not rocket science; that's pretty straightforward. He picked up that schooling from his dad, who was a developer in Queens; and now Trump is a developer around the world. There's nothing wrong with that; and it clearly shows that he's got some smarts—he's intelligent. The question is, does he have experience in the role that he's now going to play, as President of the major power of the world? I don't think he has it at this point; so it could go several ways.

If you look at his—you just mentioned Mnuchin for Secretary of the Treasury—he's got a few wing nuts in his Cabinet; there's no question about that—

more than one. They make statements at variance from his statements; and what he's instructed them to do—which is pretty clever—is that they should accurately give their views. They don't have to parrot his particular outlook. His particular outlook doesn't have any depth at this point in time; but there's two things. It can get really bad with the wing nuts taking over the administration; or, he may mature to the point where when a Cabinet member does something and gets him in trouble, that will attack his ego. Let me tell you, from my judgment, the biggest asset we have with Trump is the fact that he's got an out-sized ego; out-sized worldwide ego. That ego brings about a discipline on him, because he's got to defend himself. Here's the example that I see, which is very optimistic; maybe more so. He keeps talking about China, but also, he keeps talking about his guiding principle which is, to make a deal, to arrive at something concrete and positive. That's all well and good. With respect to China, I think his ego will understand that the biggest deal in the world that he could make, which will nurture his out-sized ego, is a deal with China to join China on the Silk Road project. That's the biggest deal that I see in the world right now; and as soon as he understands that, he'll latch on to that and take possession of it and take credit for it, and thereby join China and Russia and the BRICS in this colossal global deal which is to raise the economic level of all the peoples in the world.

What argues against that is his jingoistic attitude that the United States has got to be Number One. That's a very dangerous course to take, and of course, that's what we've been taking for the last 50 years. What's led us to the mess that we're in today, is that when we put ourselves unilaterally as Number One in the world, commanding everything in that direction, what we do is we beggar thy neighbor in the world, and that's the tragedy of what we've been doing in our foreign policy for the last 50 years. So now, what is Trump going to do? He could do something great; he could do something ridiculous and inconsequential, jumping all over with his wing nut Cabinet. That would be a missed opportunity. What will happen is, if he does pursue the nega-

> **With respect to the foreign policy, that's a whole other area. Clearly, Trump will solve the problem that was created by Obama and Hillary. Had she won, we'd probably be going to war with Russia… we're going to back away from that; and Russia, Putin, if he can develop a personal relationship with Trump, Putin can help educate him on an equal basis…**

tive, I think that there may be enough reasonableness in the world—particularly among the BRICS and others—that would limit that; wouldn't let that get out of hand, I hope. And it's a lot of hope.

What it comes down to is, right now don't worry about his inaugural speech. Six months from now, it will be inconsequential. What will be consequential, will be what they specifically do in terms of policy and interaction with foreign nations. There are two elements; there's his domestic element, and I just hope that he does throw the resources to refurbish the American infrastructure, which is a mess. The last time I was in New York, I came off the Triborough Bridge down on the East Side. I used to be a taxi cab driver in New York City, so you can imagine what age has done to me when I'm not sure east and west. But the East Side Highway was like a Third World country; it was terrible. This is in New York, the mother city of the world. We've let it get into such disrepair; and this is the situation right across the country. Just refurbishing the United States will bring about the employment level that he wants to bring about; because there's just so much to do. Now it's the question of moving the resources in that direction; that's the domestic program which we hope he will implement. I think he will, because he's made his bellwether jobs.

With respect to the foreign policy, that's a whole other area. Clearly, he'll solve the problem that was created by Obama and Hillary. Had she won, we'd probably be going to war with Russia, which is just a ridiculous, tragic situation if that would have come to pass. So, we're going to back away from that; and Russia, Putin, if he can develop a personal relationship with Trump, Putin can help educate him on an equal basis, not a paternalistic way, but on an equal basis. Putin is very clever in that regard; and he could ameliorate the situation between the United States under Trump's leadership, and China under Xi's leadership. Putin could pave the way in trying to persuade Trump that his program domestically—which is to refurbish our society—not go back to what it was in the old days; just refurbish and bring it up to speed with the most modern

Neocons Robert Kagan and Victoria Nuland, with Italian Ambassador Aldo Amati.

Flickr/Italy in US

technology possible. So, he could do that; and he will do that, in my mind.

What we've got to do is translate that goal domestically into an international goal, and that's where him joining China and the BRICS onto the Silk Road program around the world comes in; raising the economic standards of the people worldwide.

Will Trump do that? I think that the odds are that he will. What will mitigate against that, is, of course, the neo-cons—and he's got a couple of neo-cons in his Cabinet. But the real neo-cons, Victoria Nuland and her husband and that ilk—the neo-cons who took us into an invasion in Iraq—they're still around out there. And by and large, they are represented by mainstream media. Keep in mind, the problem that we have is the military-industrial complex and Wall Street controlling our government, along with Israel; controlling our government lock, stock, and barrel. So, will Trump go along with that? His son-in-law is going to be his main advisor; who apparently is religious, and so that's going to play out in a certain kind of way.

What's interesting from a political science point of view, which is certainly my point of view, is how this is going to play out. It could move in various directions, but one thing will be the lodestar of it all, and that is the President's personal ego and his sense of worth of himself and what he can accomplish. That is the biggest asset we have working on what we hope will come about.

With respect to a defined paradigm and principle—I think how quickly will Trump mature and understand what's really going on, I think that's not necessary. What is important for him is to act on what *is* necessary and what is going on and what the choices are; right now it's bifurcated. Which way will he go? Circumstances will dictate that, so it's how the wing nuts in his cabinet will act, foolishly or intelligently, and if they act foolishly, it will impact upon him and his ego, and how he will react to that remains to be seen.

I just want to have a cautionary note that I personally believe that the military-industrial complex and Wall Street control our society, not just our government, control our society, and they can be very dangerous. I'm happy that Trump is keeping his own personal security system that he's paying for, enmeshing that with the security system of the Presidency. He is well aware of the fact that if he gets too far off the reservation, it would not be that difficult a thing to assassinate him.

These are all the things that are in front of us that are going to play out. The least informed facet of this is going to be mainstream media. They're just on a witch hunt, ego trip, neo-con—trying to make the case for the rationale of the outsized military capability that we have, and we don't need that. Will Trump change that? He hasn't said he will; in fact, just the opposite, he feels that we should build up our military even more. That may not be possible if we pursue the Silk Road globally and if we pursue the equivalent of the Silk Road domestically. That is my take on it.

I don't think anybody can make any formed conclusions as to which way he'll go, but I think it's important to underscore what Lyndon and Helga have said, that at this point in time it's a waste of time to over-parse every little word he makes. He's still under the aura of the campaign and the success of his campaign, and that's why he continues to articulate the same thing over and over again. Here again, he's an intelligent person and he will develop; which way, that's the question. I leave it at that. That's the big question. What door will he open and go through? Thank you.

President Trump Must Propose a Unified Mission to Explore and Develop Space

by Kesha Rogers

The author is a former candidate and Democratic nominee for the 22nd Congressional District of Texas in 2010-2012, and a former candidate for the U.S. Senate in 2014.

Jan. 23—President Trump must immediately develop and propose to the nation a unified mission dedicated to exploring and developing space.

Man creates his own future through discoveries of higher and more powerful principles than those he wielded before. Our species is a mighty geological force, with power to sustain, change, and develop itself and its environment, unlike any other species. The extent of this power was less evident in the Middle Ages and even into the 18th century.

In his Inaugural Address, President Trump stated,

We stand at the birth of a new millennium, ready to unlock the mysteries of space, to free the Earth from the miseries of disease, and to harness the energies, industries, and technologies of tomorrow.

These cannot be merely nice words. The question is, What is required to meet such a challenge and to harness the great potential before us? Fusion power development and human exploration of space are the necessary twin drivers of human progress at this time. The development of space is not just a choice among various policy initiatives, but

the basis for advancing human progress for the long term, throughout our Solar system.

Thus, the immediate action required of President Trump is to define a unified national mission dedicated to the exploration of space, starting with the development of the Moon, and including the harnessing of its unique fusion energy resource, helium-3, for the benefit of the United States and the whole world.

China is already opening the door for a future of fusion energy through its Chang'e 4 and Chang'e 5 exploration missions. The United States cannot be left behind by ignoring this progress while floundering about with individual pet projects.

Fusion and Space Development

The path for United States leadership in space exploration and development was laid out in depth by

NASA/Pat Rawlings

Lunar mining facility extracts oxygen from resource-rich volcanic soil of eastern Mare Serenitatis.

Krafft Ehricke in the early 1980s, in his "Five Stage Lunar Development Program." First, we examine the Moon from Earth. Second, we examine the Moon from lunar orbit, consider the optimal site for an industrial base, and establish automated laboratories and pilot facilities on the surface. Third, we locate the best spot on the Moon for an initial industrial base, and establish it there. Fourth, from this base, we establish a larger industrial zone that can return resources to Earth while expanding across the Moon. And fifth, we expand and diversify from this initial base to create a translunar space-faring civilization.[1] China is already doing this, and the United States has to catch up after years of decay.

Krafft Ehricke understood that—

Courtesy of the late Krafft Ehricke

Winter in Selenopolis, where Earth seasons are artificially replicated. On the left, Hall of the Astronauts.

Space opens new horizons beyond Earth and offers new beginnings in ways we can manage this precious planet. It offers noble aspirations, opportunities for creative action, for bringing the human family closer together and contributing to a better future for all.[2]

Ehricke's lunar development plan lays the basis for a viable space platform *and* the economic foundation for a better life on Earth, by enabling, for example, a fusion economy—fusion power development is the fourth of Lyndon LaRouche's four needed laws to make the United States great once again.

The advances of a fusion economy will require a completely new set of international relations around the planet and will increase the creative and productive powers of mankind throughout the Solar system.

Fusion technology—the fusion torch—will separate waste into its constituent elements that can therefore be reused repeatedly. Fusion technologies will benefit all sectors of our economy, enabling us to increase the productivity of our labor force as spin-off technologies are introduced into sectors such as healthcare, agriculture, manufacturing, energy, defense, transportation, and resource development.

That is how fusion technology will open up massive, untapped resources that the United States can use to employ our citizens, grow stronger, build relationships with other nations, and become a leader in the world that other nations will respect, learn from, and collaborate with, in achieving the common aims of mankind.

Every nation that develops a mastery of fusion technology will free itself from the burden of limited resources, and enter into a new era of unprecedented wealth creation for its citizens.

In this way, the exploration and colonization of nearby space, and the development of the technologies required to do so, become a vehicle through which the United States will again inspire the world as we increasingly meet the common needs and aspirations of mankind. We can realize the vision of our great President John F. Kennedy, who said, at Rice University on Sept. 12, 1962,

---

1. The five steps are elaborated in Ehricke's article, "Lunar Industrialization and Settlement—Birth of Polyglobal Civilization," reprinted in Marsha Freeman, *Krafft Ehricke's Extraterrestrial Imperative* (Apogee Books, 2008), pp. 259-287. The article is also available on the Lunar and Planetary Institute website at http://www.lpi.usra.edu/publications/books/lunar_bases/LSBchapter12.pdf pp. 827-855. For a graphic depiction of the five steps, see Fusion Energy Foundation, *Beam Defense: An Alternative to Nuclear Destruction* (Fallbrook, CA: Aero Publishers, 1983), p. 144.
2. Krafft Ehricke, "A Case for Space" (1970), in Marsha Freeman, *op. cit.*, p. 204.

For the eyes of the world now look into space, to the Moon and to the planets beyond, and we have vowed that we shall not see it governed by a hostile flag of conquest, but by a banner of freedom and peace. We have vowed that we shall not see space filled with weapons of mass destruction, but with instruments of knowledge and understanding.

A Unified Mission

Today, China is leading the world in fulfilling mankind's extraterrestrial imperative, with steady progress in its lunar program as seen in its lunar probe, the Chang'e 5 mission, planned to be launched this November aboard the heavy lift Long March 5 rocket. This mission

9ifly.cn

Rollout of China's Long March 5 heavy-lift rocket, Oct. 28, 2016.

will be followed by the Chang'e 4 lander mission in 2018, executing mankind's first soft landing on the far side of the Moon.

The United States must join in these efforts, and must remove all limitations to the needed cooperation. China and the United States must become partners in the development of space, and no one and nothing must stand in the way of that. We must bring about a unified human mission that establishes a completely new view of the human species in the Solar system and the Galaxy, defined not by the compartmentalization of space exploration and settlement, but by a new, unprecedented level of cooperation on Earth.

President Trump must act for a unified mission now.

III. A Dialogue of Civilizations

Schiller Institute Martin Luther King Weekend Celebration in New York City

Below is a transcript of Dennis Speed's introduction to the Jan. 14 portion of the Jan. 14-15 Martin Luther King conference and concert. This is the video link to the introduction by Speed, and the presentations by Helga Zepp-LaRouche and Ben Wang.

Dennis Speed: My name is Dennis Speed, and on behalf of the Schiller Institute, I want to welcome everyone today to our conference to inaugurate the New Paradigm, and to advance the dialogue of civilizations. You could also refer to today's proceedings as the poetic principle in politics and art. It's a two-day congress that we're holding; we're having a conference today, and a concert tomorrow in Brooklyn.

These events are embedded, this dialogue is embedded in that process that's happening in the United States—the Presidential transition. The poet Percy Shelley, in the conclusion of his *A Defense of Poetry,* asserted that poets are the "unacknowledged legislators of the world."

Today, we seek and require that poetry, the poetic principle, be acknowledged at the necessary basis for statecraft and for a dialogue of civilizations.

HELGA ZEPP-LAROUCHE

Inaugurating a New Paradigm: A Dialogue of Civilizations

This is a transcript of Helga Zepp-LaRouche's address to the Schiller Institute conference which took place in New York City on Jan. 14, 2017. Zepp-LaRouche was introduced by Dennis Speed.

Dennis Speed: The Schiller Institute was created as an attempt to introduce that [poetic] principle into East-West relations back in 1983. But there was not really a vision in the U.S. government at that time for such a thing to occur. So Helga LaRouche, on her own, created and initiated that vision. This higher cultural idea was the actual basis, however, of what today you know as the World Land-Bridge, or the New Silk Road, or many other forms of proposals which are often referred to as economic proposals, or political proposals.

But they are really policies for a new world cultural platform, and a higher conception of economics that would flow from that higher cultural conception. The General Welfare clause of the American Constitution is completely compatible with the concept of "win-win" cooperation that underlies the idea of the New Silk Road and the One Belt, One Road, which are the ideas, for example, that President Xi Jinping of China has been discussing. But, we need a cultural Silk Road as well.

For the last twenty years, Helga has been known as the Silk Road Lady because of the work that she did in China and in her speaking at a conference that happened at that time in Beijing in June of 1996. Now more than ever, her contribution and the contribution that we made with respect to this idea of a dialogue of civilizations, will be the necessary basis for this new cultural paradigm. And so, it's always my honor to introduce the founder of the Schiller Institutes, Helga LaRouche.

Above: Campaigners for BREXIT outside the House of Commons in London, November 2016.

SPECIAL REPORT

DONALD TRUMP ELECTED
45TH PRESIDENT OF THE UNITED STATES

SENATE
PENNSYLVANIA

	48%	2,892,8
PAT TOOMEY	48%	2,892,8
KATIE MCGINTY	47%	2,793,0

Right: The final word of CBS News on election night after the Donald Trump victory.

Not an American but a Global Process

Now this has everything to do with the fact that this is not an internal-American incident alone, but the absolutely surprising election for many—for most people—of Donald Trump, is actually part of a global process which is underway, and which is not going to stop until the reasons and causes for this process—which you can actually call a global revolution—are removed.

Remember that the Soviet Union only collapsed a quarter of a century ago, which is not a very long time in terms of real history. At that time, Francis Fukuyama actually said this was the end of history, and that the Western liberal democracy model has been demonstrated to be victorious over communism. He indicated that in the future, there will no longer be a fight between ideas. Instead, the future will be characterized only by economic and technical problems, and therefore, it will be relatively boring.

He was obviously absolutely wrong, because this period of history, which I would say started with the collapse of the Soviet Union, and which led to what we call "globalization," is coming to an end. Or, has come to an end already. Obviously, that process really started with the broken promises of the United States and others not to expand NATO to the Russian border, which subsequently was broken many times. The recent deployment of U.S. and NATO troops and military equipment to the Russian borders is just the latest example of that.

So, that breakdown started practically immediately, following the disintegration of the Soviet Union. But the real escalation of the financial dimension of this globalization occurred with the repeal of the Glass-Steagall Act in 1999, leading to the absolutely unrestricted speculation which then subsequently led to the crash of 2008, and which has now brought the world to

Helga Zepp-LaRouche: Well, ladies and gentlemen, I'm very happy to greet you in this way, via video and "Hangout." But before I speak about this subject which Dennis mentioned—the dialogue of cultures—I want to briefly situate the need for such a dialogue of cultures in the context of the current strategic situation, because we are living in such extremely dramatic times.

I think, given the fact that you are in New York and in the United States, I don't have to tell you that the situation around the incoming new President can only be described as absolutely hysterical. I have never seen such a thing in my lifetime—that you have a newly elected President, who actually will come into the White House in all likelihood in six days—but the hysteria of the mainstream neo-liberal media and a large part of the political establishment on both sides of the Atlantic have not calmed down. It seems that they still do not accept the fact that there will be a new President.

You Tube video

Obama's Director of National Intelligence, James R. Clapper.

Obama's CIA director, John Brennan.

C-SPAN video

FBI Director James Comey.

the verge of another such crash, which will be much bigger and more dangerous.

What has happened in the recent period, is that the people who were the victims of these changes—whereby the billionaires became richer, the poor became poorer, and the middle class increasingly vanished in many countries—there has been a revolt against that. Because the people who came to the conclusion that with this system of globalization, they would not have a future—they started to revolt; and the first massive demonstration of this revolt was the Brexit, the exit of Great Britain from the EU in June of last year.

The next major manifestation of that was the vote for Trump. Especially the people in the American "rust belt," and other areas where people felt they had no future with this system, voted against the tradition of Bush-Cheney, Obama, and therefore against Hillary as a clear continuation of that policy. Then, a couple of weeks later, the "no" to the referendum in Italy against the EU bureaucracy was an expression of the same process. It will continue, because this year—2017—there will be many elections in Europe, where you will see the same kind of dynamic in process.

The trans-Atlantic establishment was completely shocked. First about the Brexit, then about the Trump victory. It was very clear that from day one, they did not accept these developments. It was quite amazing to see that they expressed shock, they expressed dismay. They used unbelievable language against the elected President of the United States. They did not accept it, but they also did not want to look at the reasons why this election result had occurred.

Therefore, they decided to replace the truth with a new narrative, that Russia stole the election by hacking the DNC, by hacking Podesta. Naturally what they didn't want people to be reminded of any more, was that if anybody stole the election, then it was the DNC stealing the election from Bernie Sanders—but that was sort of pushed under the carpet. Instead you had the non-stop accusations that Russia hacked the U.S. election process. That it was Russia favoring Trump, and therefore Russia really stole the election; which is quite an admission all by itself, and quite ludicrous. But that is what they decided to go with.

Naturally, there was never any evidence presented for this. Then, parallel to the Russian hacking story as such, a British agent, formerly of MI6—British intelligence—Christopher Steele, started to put together a 35-page report with unbelievable allegations against Trump. I do not even want to give it the honor of repeating it here—it's totally ludicrous. Again, no evidence. This report was already available to all the media in the election period—September, October; it was given to the FBI, but nobody touched it, because it was so clear to everybody that there was absolutely no evidence for it.

So then, eventually the same paper was given by McCain to the FBI again, and only after Trump had said that he believed Julian Assange of WikiLeaks, more than the U.S. intelligence services.

All hell broke loose, and the three intelligence chiefs—Clapper, Brennan, and Comey—first briefed the U.S. Senate, then President Obama, and finally Trump, with the so-called "evidence" of this Russian hacking. They made a 2-page summary of the 35 pages of this report by Christopher Steele, and added that into the material that they gave to Trump. With that particular act, they gave this completely ridiculous report the authority of being a product of the intelligence. Then, CNN published it, followed by the internet firm BuzzFeed, and then all rest of the media. The story broke out in the open. This occurred exactly the evening before the first press conference by Donald Trump.

Obviously, this is an unbelievable story. even French intelligence people, like Eric Denécé, who is an official of French intelligence, said it is simply that the American establishment fears that a big clean-out will come with the new administration, and they will lose their privileges and economic benefits. So therefore, they oppose it; but there is absolutely no evidence for it.

PIB

Indian Prime Minister Narendra Modi hosted the five BRICS heads of State at the BRICS Summit in Goa, India, on Oct. 16, 2016. Modi is shown here, at that summit, with Russian President Vladimir Putin (left) and Chinese President Xi Jinping (right).

The Deeper Level

I think there is a deeper level to this whole thing, and that is the fact that what Donald Trump is threatening, is the unipolar world which the neo-cons and the neo-liberals have been building since the collapse of the Soviet Union. They backed regime change, color revolution, and wars based on lies against all countries that would not submit to the idea of a unipolar world run by the British and the American governments.

Trump, as you know, has promised that he would remedy the relationship with Russia; and despite some tensions, there are also signs, that he may actually have very good cooperation with China, especially since he wants to attain a $1 trillion investment in rebuilding the American infrastructure. He has already received offers from China to cooperate. He had an excellent discussion with the CEO of Alibaba, the large e-commerce firm of China. He met with Jack Ma, and they agreed to together invest another $1 trillion. So the signs are actually quite good.

If the United States cooperates with Russia, and has a decent relationship with China, then naturally the entire game plan to have this unipolar world—or call it globalization, which is just another word for the Anglo-American financial empire—would go out of the window. That is why they are trying to undo this election of Donald Trump. You can see very clearly that this is a direct intervention by the British.

Therefore, it's not a question of party against party. Or it's not a question of nation against nation. It is the old dying paradigm of the British Empire—if you equate that with globalization—clearly reacting to the emergence of the New Paradigm. That New Paradigm, however, is already very strong, and is moving very rapidly.

China has initiated this New Paradigm with this New Silk Road policy, and has offered "win-win" cooperation to all countries who want to cooperate. Already, more than 70 nations are engaged with China in huge infrastructure projects, projects of scientific cooperation, the most advanced technologies, space cooperation, and other such things. It's already twelve times the size of the Marshall Plan of the postwar period. Every day, new exciting breakthroughs are being reported. On Tuesday of this past week, the first standard-gauge railway between Djibouti and Addis Abeba started to carry passengers. This 750 km rail line was inaugurated Oct. 5 last year, and carried freight for three months for purposes of testing.

China has also begun a feasibility study of the Lake Chad project, Transaqua, to replenish Lake Chad, where the volume of water has now shrunk to 10% of its previous amount. This is endangering the lives of about 40 million people living in the Chad basin. This project will reverse that decline, and fill Lake Chad with water coming from the Congo River area, by using about 3-4% of the unused water of the Congo River, which flows into the Atlantic Ocean.

The project will not take water from the mouth of the Congo, but will take it from the tributaries of the Congo River. In that way, using gravity over a 500-meter drop in elevation, Lake Chad can be refilled. This will affect the lives of twelve nations. It will create a navigable waterway, it will provide hydropower, and it will open up large amounts of land for irrigation and agriculture. It is a fantastic development.

Similarly, there are reports that the Kra Canal, which will shorten the trip between the Pacific and the [Indian] Oceans, and which will be one of the absolute hubs for three billion people in Southeast Asia and South Asia, is also now going to be built. These are all projects we have been fighting for, for 20, 30, or 40 years; so all of this is extremely positive and good.

So-Called Clash of Civilizations

Together with this ridiculous Fukuyama story about the end of history, 25 years ago, you also had Samuel Huntington predicting that even after the collapse of the communist system, you would still have a clash of civilizations. He claimed that the axioms of the different religions and civilizations were so different, that there never could be unity and harmony for the human race.

He wrote an absolutely absurd book called *Clash of Civilizations*. That is equally as wrong as Fukuyama was wrong; because with the win-win economic cooperation of the New Silk Road, you have the possibility of having a dialogue of cultures on the highest level. That is exactly what the Schiller Institute is promoting with conferences like this. The basic idea is that if all the people were just to know the most beautiful expressions of the high phases of the other culture, they would love the other culture, because they would feel so enriched, and recognize that it is a beauty that we have many cultures.

It would be very boring if there were only one civilization. In particular, the Western liberal one is not exactly attractive. Therefore, if you look at the Confucian tradition in China, Mencius, the literati paintings, or if you look at the Vedic writings, or the Gupta Sanskrit drama tradition in India, the Indian renaissance of Tagore, Sri Aurobindo, or if you look at the Italian Renaissance, or the German Classical period in music, in literature—especially in music from Bach to Beethoven to Brahms—all these are contributions to universal history. Once every nation knows the best expressions of the other one, I'm absolutely certain that all conflicts will absolutely disappear, and we will have a rich, universal culture consisting of many national expressions and traditions, but still be united by universal principles of art and science.

Now, the other dimension which must come to this dialogue of cultures, or dialogue of civilizations, is a look into the future. Not only back to the best traditions, but a look to where mankind should be in 100 years, in 1,000 years from now. There, it is very clear that the natural next phase of evolution is space—travel, research, cooperation, and colonization of space. If you look at the long arc of evolution, life developed from the oceans with the help of photosynthesis, to move to land. You had higher forms of species developing with higher forms of energy-flux density in their metabolisms. Eventually, man arrived. Man started to move inland from the rivers and ocean coasts, with the help of infrastructure, and opened up the landlocked areas. Now, we are at that point where the New Silk Road, as it becomes the World Land-Bridge, is completing that phase of the evolutionary development.

So, the natural next phase of evolution is the development of nearby space in the first phase, and then further space travel as we develop the technologies to do so, with the help of fusion energy and similar technologies. Man will expand in space. Then we will no longer be just an Earth-bound species, but we will be a cosmopolitical species, if you want. That will then lead to a completely new knowledge about the identity of the human species.

We are in a period of real epochal change—a New Paradigm—where I am absolutely certain mankind is about to become adult. Wars will absolutely be a question of the past. Wars will be not worthy of the beautiful human species which has so much creativity to still discover. We are just at the embryonic stage of mankind.

Anyway, I just wanted to share these ideas with you, because if Trump sticks to his guns, if he can defeat this assault against him, and if you can help to bring the United States into the New Paradigm—working with Russia, and working with China—the future will be absolutely fantastic! That is really what I wanted to tell you.

BEN WANG

Anticipating the Spring to Come

This is an edited transcript of an address by Dr. Ben Wang to the Manhattan Schiller Institute Conference, Jan. 14, 2017.

Dennis Speed: Ben Wang is many things. He's an award winning, published writer, translator, author of multiple books on Chinese Classical literature, primarily poetry; senior lecturer in languages and humanities at China Institute, and many, many other things. He's lectured everywhere, and teaches at the United Nations—you name it. But, the most important thing about this gentleman that I think is important, is his *love* for what he does. And I'm not going to say more about it, because I think you're going to see him express it. The actual topic, let me just say, as I see it, is "The Soul of an Ancient Culture: Classical Poetry and Literati Painting of China." This is something he's going to be lecturing on in the subsequent weeks, and people can find out other information about that at the table. So, Ben.

EIRNS/Jason Ross

Dr. Ben Wang

Dr. Ben Wang: Now, I'm going to veer away from realism. One of my favorite writers, poets, and playwrights, is America's great Tennessee Williams. Blanche DuBois, one of the greatest characterizations by Williams, says: "I don't want realism. I want magic." But of course, life is inseparable from realism, but I'll try to veer away.

So today, I'm going to talk about the poetic lines written almost exactly 1,300 years ago. (I was counting when I was sitting there.)

In the Chinese language, in Chinese culture we have a saying, "keep revealing, keep going over the old, and the new will come to you." And one of my favorite writers of the 20th Century, Muriel Spark, writes, famously, in *The Prime of Miss Jean Brodie:* "The glory of the past is the inspiration of the future." So even though I'm talking about a dead poet's lines, I feel they last forever. To the Chinese literary critics, every good Classical Chinese poem, every line, might have eighteen layers of underlying images. So as I'm getting older, the four lines in total that I'm going to introduce were the lines that I studied when I was eight and nine years old! And now I'm eighty, and I'm still talking about it, because over the years, I dug up many underlying images which I couldn't understand when I was four.

I warned Dennis when I came in—Dennis had told me that I had forty minutes to talk about whatever I wanted. Outside I didn't say anything, because I'm a guest, but inside, I was saying "forty minutes only? These four lines would take me four *hours* to do!" And then I looked at you, the ladies and gentlemen, and I'm not trying to kiss you up; I really meant it, I looked at you and sized you up and I figured you out, and I said, "These guys could stay with me for at least four hours for these four lines!" [laughter] Of course, I'm not going to do that,—don't be scared! This one is old, but still my hearing is good. I already promised Dennis that I would behave myself. Well, China Institute, and other places, I warn them first.

So, because of the time constraint, I would like to

read about the poet whose works I'm going to introduce. It's on the screen, the first page, please. His name is Li Bai, and this is an excerpted version of a book which is to be published soon; it's at my publisher's:

Li Bai of China's great Tang dynasty, most famous for its poetry, is the most celebrated poet of the period, and in Chinese literature, earned the reverend sobriquet of "Celestial of Poetry" from the Chinese readers and scholars over the centuries. Li Bai's distinction lies in that he brings a special eloquence and bravura to his poetic works with an exceptionally notable flow and grandeur during an era when lack of them would be an exception.

Li Bai's poetry on the whole is vivacious, hopeful, and philosophical in outlook. This special transporting quality that is featured in all his works, appears to grow out of this outlook that he held regarding life and art. His pursuit of spiritual freedom and beauty in life, his divine communion with Nature, as well as his keen sensitivity to the Chinese language that is a unique blending of music and picture—in that spoken Chinese is singing and written Chinese is painting—so because of this I would like to think the Chinese language is eminently suited for poetry, for its concision. All these elements join forces to contribute in establishing him as a poet, peerless among his peers, a master of all masters.

Without further ado, I would like to introduce the two selected lines. During the Tang dynasty, two poetic forms flourished. Pentasyllabic poems and heptasyllabic poems, because the Chinese language is a monosyllabic language, in that every character has only one syllable, so when I say, "pentasyllabic" that means five characters per line; when I say "heptasyllabic" poem, that means seven characters per line. Either they are quatrains or regulated verse, which means two quatrains put together, eight lines in total. And they are always an even number, even though the number of each line is an odd number; but the total number of a poem must be an even number so they balance out. To the Chinese everything must be balanced because of this *yin* and *yang* union, perfect union between *yin* and *yang*.

Way back in ancient times, Chinese poetry—I'm talking about between 1100 and 500 B.C.—all the poems as they are printed out in the *Book of Songs*, translated by the great Arthur Waley, were written in four characters per line, quadrisyllabic. But then, quickly during the Han dynasty, which began about 200 B.C., the Chinese started to produce pentasyllabic poems, because by adding one character to the quadrisyllabic poems, the Chinese found there's more musicality to it—as we're doing bum, bum, bum, bum,—bum. Sounds much better than bum, bum, bum, bum.

So a student over the years suggested to me, "Teacher, actually Classical Chinese when you're reading it, it's rap!" I said, "You're right. I think rap comes from China!" [laughter] So, after a few hundred years, the bum, bum, bum, bum,—bum, some Chinese scholars, poets said, "why don't we make it seven characters? Then it's, bum, bum, bum, bum, bum, bum,—bum!" There's more of a rhythm. So pentasyllabic developed quickly developed into heptasyllabic poems. And during the Tang dynasty, in these two poetic genres, in pentasyllabic form and heptasyllabic form, poetry flourished.

We have to study these two couplets. They are selected from two poems. One is from "Tune of Clarity and Serenity," and this poem is written in the style of a ballad. I'm sure you all know, a ballad is a song. I mean, poetry is inseparable from songs, and this is written in the style of a ballad. So the tonal scheme—there are four tones in the Chinese language; two of them are high, and two of them are low. So when you are writing Classical poetry, you must abide by the high-high, low-low-high; and the second line low-low, high-high-low. So there's a perfect balance, so the high tones are the masculine force tones. They are set to characters that should logically belong in the masculine force-dominated universe; whereas the low tones should, ideally, be set to characters, pictures, that should logically belong to the feminine force-dominated universe. So the tonal scheme is very strict.

But in the ballad style, the tonal scheme is not rigorous. So the first two lines—this is from a poem written in the style of ballad—so the tonal scheme is not that rigorously composed.

Before I go on, I must emphasize one important fact, which is, it seems that the Chinese writer, composer, poet—they seem to be quite impossible to be separated from nature. Everything is metaphor, metaphor, metaphor: a petal falls, that means the poet is getting old, the golden halcyon days are going. If there's a drizzle, that means a little vicissitude, or a little ache of the heart. So it's always like this. That's why when I saw the movie,

"Il Postino," when I heard the word "*Metafore*"—and I said, "metaphor, yes, Chinese poetry is all about metaphor." Because to the Chinese, to come right out, to talk about "I, you, me, I'm suffering…," is just so vulgar! So everything is borrowed. A flower, a fleecy cloud, a piece of cloud floating, and everything connects with human life, with human existence.

Tune of Clarity and Serenity

With this in mind, we'll study, we'll look at this. The first line—first let me read the two lines. See if you, without understanding a thing, see if you feel anything about it (see **Figure 1**).

yún xiǎng yīshang huā xiǎng róng
(cloud think clothes robe flower think face)
chūn fēng fú kǎn lù huá nóng
(Spring wind caress doorsill dew essence rich)

Only fourteen syllables because it's a heptasyllabic couplet. So the first character is "cloud." Now, every Chinese character is picture. In other words, there is no Chinese character, not one character that is not a picture; a picture of nature—we put them together. And so, seemingly at first glance, the Chinese language is totally visceral. But when it gets to the poetic level, then the visceral joins forces with the cerebral: Then beauty and poetry occur, happen. So the first character *yún* is "cloud." The top, do you see the dots and windowpanes, that's rain coming down. If rain is coming down, you see clouds are hovering, dark clouds, so the first character is a picture in which the top part is the rain, the bottom part is the cloud.

And the second character *xiǎng* is "heart." The bottom is the radical meaning, the root of the character which is the heart. Now, the Chinese heart is the mind, because in ancient times there were two things the Chinese didn't know the truth of: One, is when human beings emote, it is our mind that is working; but the Chinese thought it was the heart, because when you are about to cry you feel a little squeeze of the muscles here, near the area of the heart. But you don't get a headache! So the Chinese didn't know—and we feel the palpitating of the heart, the beating of the heart; but the brain, inside it's still, it doesn't move. If it starts to move, you know you're about to die or something! [laughter] So the Chinese always go one step below. So what to the Western people is the mind, to the Chinese is the heart.

The word in English, "heartbreak," guess what it is in Chinese? Literally translated, it would be "intestines broken." You say, "that sounds disgusting!" But think

FIGURE 1

A heptasyllabic couplet
(from *Tune of Clarity and Serenity*)
by Li Bai (761-763)

雲想衣裳花想容

yún xiǎng yīshang huā xiǎng róng

cloud think clothes robe flower think face

春風拂檻露華濃　（743）

chūn fēng　fú　kǎn　lù　huá nóng

spring wind caress doorsill dew essence rich

about it. How is the body part, heart, different from intestines? They're all body parts; you know, we feel like "my guts are rending, are breaking"; here, guts are close to the intestines. So when we hear "intestines broken," we feel, oh, that's so poetic. [laughter] But literally translated, you'd say "this is disgusting, I fail to see any beauty in this poem! What are these intestines…?" So we always translate "intestines broken" as "heartbroken"; but actually it's not correct. But then, no translation is the real thing. As the famous Roy Campbell, a very great man of letters of the 20th Century and the early part of the century—he was a poet and a writer, and also a philosopher—he says something about translation, and—no offense to all the ladies here, no offense, I hope—he says, "Translations, like wives, are never faithful if they are the least bit attractive." [laughter] And even though it doesn't sound very respectful to women, yet I tend to agree with him. I'm so sorry. I know I'm totally socially wrong, but I didn't say it, Roy Campbell said it.

So, the second character has the heart on the bottom. Unfortunately, I don't have a white board so that I could show you the evolution of this picture, how it started out a heart-looking character form, and then it went through linear changes throughout the centuries until it finally got to look how it looks now, the second character of the first line from the left. The bottom is "heart." So whenever you see that, that means that the character has something to do with the mind or the heart. So the second character is the heart radical, and the top component—I cannot get into details because of the time—the top component means "have a relationship between two"—either two people or one person to an inanimate object. It means to think about something, to miss something, to yearn for something, to wish for something; or romantically yearning, or "I think about you"; or just simply, without emotions, "I think . . ." it's going to rain, or that kind of "thinking." So one picture can have a thousand meanings. This is really the case with the Chinese language. I had to put down one English word underneath to give you an idea, so I put down "yearn." But it can be "think," "wish," "want," a lot of English words.

So, the clouds, the first character is cloud or clouds; and then "think," or wish or yearn for.

And then the third character, you see the top dot, in the old days, is the head of a person, and then his shoulder, and then his robes—It's not difficult for you to imagine the aesthetic sense for the Chinese people. We feel that clothes have to be large, clothes have to be loose in order to be good-looking; I think it has something to do with the way ancient Chinese people were, because of the diet system. Most ancient Chinese people were very thin because of the diet, and they liked to wear, especially if they're important people, they like to wear very loose clothes in order to look bigger and more important. Does that make any sense? So the third character is "robe," clothes, or dress, any clothes.

And in the third character, do you see this character "clothes" appears on the bottom of this character—the fourth? It means "robe," "dress" and "robe,"—*yīshang*—put together it's a general word for "apparel" in general—clothes, dresses, including the robe, or the cape that you wear that gives a flowing effect.

And then the fifth character is "blossom," "flower." And the sound *huā* [very open sound], look at my mouth—*huā*. Because the ancient Chinese saw grass, it's just grass; all of a sudden, Spring comes, warm weather comes and it blooms and opens up, and the sound is *huā*! You see how visceral the language is; in the picture, the top is the radical which is "grass." In the old days, it's "grass." The bottom is "transformation," or "chemistry." So the ancient Chinese didn't know what happened: All of a sudden, the warm weather comes, this grass opens up chemically, transforms into a flower, the tip of the grass. So it's grass, as the radical; the bottom is transform. The grass has transformed itself into a blossom . . . so the tone, the sound, is *huā*, it's a high tone. Can you do it? You're good! You'll come to study Chinese with me!

And then, the second character is repeated, which is actually a poetic taboo to have two of the same character appear in the same line. It doesn't take great imagi-nation to understand this point. Here, too, if you use a verb in the same sentence repeatedly, it's very boring. "I like you. I like your brother, I like your sister," you just get so bored. Change—I'm fond of him, or I love your mom, or I adore your father. You change a word—instead of "I like your father, I like your mother. . ." So particularly when you are composing a poem it's almost a taboo, a major *faux pas,* to have two of the same character be so close to each other. So obviously the poet is doing this intentionally to emphasize this "yearn for." And the last character is "face." The classical Chinese character for "face."

So put together: cloud, yearn for, dress and robe, and blossoms, yearn for, face.

At this point I must tell you a little bit about the historical background of the composition of the poem, including these two lines. During the Tang dynasty, poetry flourished, so Li Bai was summoned by the Emperor Illumination—this is my loose translation—Emperor Illumination. He was considered one of the towering emperors in the history of Chinese literature.

So on a Spring day during the Tang dynasty, the Chinese developed the peonies; and peonies became a very fashionable and trendy flower. Everybody liked peonies and they come in different colors. So in early Spring, the second or the third lunar month of the calendar, around late April, the peonies were in full bloom, and the Emperor said to the head eunuch, "get Li Bai over here," because he was the resident poet in the palace, which was a rare honor. But what did Li Bai do with this honor? He abused it; he drank all day long—none of his favorite things. Guess what the other thing is? Beauty. Beauty in nature and beauty in a person, namely, women. So he idled away his days in his indulgence in these two—wine and women. He had no time to compose poetry for the Emperor. He said, "I could care less. I didn't want to come, you called me. You sent for me, I didn't send for you."

The Emperor would ask about him, asking him to compose poetry. He said, "no, no, no, I'm busy having fun, enjoying *la joie de vivre*." So he's summoned to the palace and the Emperor's favorite concubine, Imperial Consort I should say, who caused the downfall of the great Tang dynasty—she was a true *femme fatale*; one of the greatest *femme fatales* in the history of China, beautiful beyond description.

So on this Spring day, peonies were in full bloom, and she was particularly lovely, at twilight time. So the Emperor sent the eunuch to fetch Li Bai; Li Bai was stone drunk already, on fine wine of course. He said,

"Don't bother me." He said to the head eunuch, "Tell the Emperor I'm busy." The eunuch said, "Busy? Doing what?" He said, "Getting drunk! Do you mind? I like my wine."

So the eunuch said, "I can't go back to the Emperor, he'll kill me! He'll order my execution! Please, please, do me a favor, I beg of you." So, Li Bai says, "Oh, what a pest! The court is beckoning me, and summoning me, and getting me to the palace, just for me to compose. I'm not a poetry composing machine, you know!" So he's mumbling his displeasure as he walked to the King and his Imperial Consort; they're in the Imperial garden appreciating the peonies blooming. And so when he got there, he was drunk and he said to the chief eunuch, "take off my boots," and he just laid down, which was totally against etiquette. Ultimately, because of his wild behavior, in the end, the Emperor nicely, kindly sent him home, saying, "you're free, go do whatever you want." He was given a lot money and then he left. He had stayed in the palace for about five years, and in the end he said, "five years too long!"

Of course, he's extremely sensitive to beauty and the peonies, and the Spring night, and the Spring moonlight, the Moon is rising, and this gorgeous Imperial Consort, she's sitting there and she and the Emperor are drinking. So, he takes one look and of course, he's impressed. And Li Bai says, "what do you want me to compose, Your Majesty?" The Emperor said, "compose a poem in praise of the beauty of my beloved." So, he said, "Hmm! OK, is the paper and the ink stone, and ink paddy prepared?" The Emperor said, "Long prepared," and everything was presented to him. So it took Li Bai a second, and he came up with this one line.

Beauty and Love

And before I go on, there are two topics, in my opinion—in my very humble opinion, as a translator, as a writer—two most challenging and difficult topics to write about, even to talk about: That is, beauty. One is beauty, beauty of a person, particularly. What do you talk about—long lashes? The color of the eyes, and the fine skin, and—we all know that. Why is that challenging? Because we know beauty, we have seen beauty, everyone, especially a person of my age. I've seen beautiful people all my life—like Dennis! [laughter] I think he's really handsome.

What's the other difficult topic, to write about, or to talk about? Love. Again, because we have all experienced that. So in order to write about beauty, the beauty of a person, or about nature—or to write about love between two people—you have to be a genius, like Mozart. Mozart is for children, or for geniuses—so says Alicia de Larrocha. So says Ben Wang.

So I think these two are the most difficult topics. So, Li Bai being Li Bai, the greatest poet in the history of Chinese literature, he sat down for few seconds; he took one look at the backdrop, and the beauty and the scent and the beauty of the blossoms and the beauty of this Imperial Consort—almost without missing a beat—he came up with this line. So I learned this line in school, when I was in my teens; the first time I read it I was about eight or nine. Teachers taught us to interpret this line as "When you see the fleeting of clouds, you think of her robes. When you see blooming, flowering blossoms, you think of her face." Which is beautiful enough. And that is the interpretation of almost all teachers and students in China.

But as I have lived for so long, more and more I feel that is not the only thing. Because in the Chinese language, as I said, human beings—to talk about human life is a little low and very vulgar, so here, the cloud is functioning, can be interpreted grammatically as being the *subject* of the line, which means: "as the clouds are flying by, and they look down, what do they see? Her robes. And the clouds are yearning for her clothes. "Why can't we be more like your robes"? So even heavenly objects are envious of her. And when the peonies are blooming, they are the subject—*huā*—they yearn to look more like her. "Why can't we look more like you"? As youthful people, human beings may think we are beautiful, but look at that face! So, the blossoms yearn for her face, as clouds are yearning for her robes.

And I think to describe a beauty in that line, and the Imperial Consort started to laugh so happily—wouldn't you, ladies here?—not only, "when we see clouds, we think of her robes, when we see a blooming flower we think of her face" but "the clouds and the flowers—they are envious of her!"

I would say there is only *one* Western counterpart, that is *Salomé*, as she is described by Oscar Wilde. Oscar Wilde wrote *Salomé* in French, and then he himself translated it into English. And how did he describe Salomé's beauty? You know Salomé from the Bible? Oscar says, "Salomé, she looks like a white rose, as it is reflected in a silver plate in the moonlight." And I think *that* can be the Western counterpart to this *yishang*. This is her face.

And the second line, the first character, Spring; the

second line starts with the first character "Spring"; second character "wind, breeze"; *fú* is "caress," "flowed by"; *kan* is "doorsill"; *lù* is "dew"; *huá* is "the essence," "the essence of dew." It's the Chinese equivalent of "the essence of perfume"; *nóng* is "rich" and *nóng*, the last character of the second line is "water" and "farming"; "water to farming," it means "rich."

So the first line is about her apparel, her clothes and her face. And the second line is about her movement. "When she moves, it's Springtime." The Spring breeze is caressing the doorsill, blowing, and the scent, the fragrance is her scent.

So the face and the robes are not enough; the second line is her movement and her scent, the scent that she emanates, this Imperial Consort. Do you see the beauty of this woman? And everything is metaphor; nothing is real.

In order to translate this poem, I cannot put—I always say to my students, to my friends, to my audience, I would say, "Classical Chinese poetry deserves annotation, but not translation. You need to explain. Otherwise you just look at the facial,— by the face. Of course, there is surface luster, but ultimately, you need a helping hand to guide you, word by word, character by character, to know the quintessence of the beauty. That's why I decided to do what I did—for you to imagine. So the translation is in a very unique but bizarre way. Actually, I did not translate. All I did was to just put the almost equivalents of those characters like that, just for you to get an idea. But once you have heard me talk, I hope it gives you something.

Passing Parrot Isle

Now the second couplet that I chose to talk about is from a poem called "Parrot Isle"; the word "passing" is what I added. This Parrot Isle is known for its natural beauty. There are a lot of beautiful parrots in the beautiful blossoms and plant life, in the Spring in particular. And I'm sure it's because it's so beautiful, that it can't last forever; nothing that beautiful can last forever. Garbo didn't last forever.

So the Parrot Isle in the 14th Century, it sank, the

FIGURE 2

Another Heptasyllabic couplet
(from *Passing Parrot Isle*)
by Li Bai (701-763)

煙開蘭葉香風暖

yān kāi lán yè xiāng fēng nuǎn

smoke/mist open orchid leaf fragrant wind warm

岸夾桃花錦浪生 （760）

àn jiā táo huā jǐn làng sheng

riverbank pressed-between peach blossom colorful brocade wave birth

isle; it's like Atlantis. So now it's almost a myth, although once it was there: It was called "Parrot Isle" [pronounces it in Chinese]. During the Tang dynasty it was there.

Obviously Li Bai was not only a great poet, a wine-lover, and an aesthete, but also he was a great traveler. He loved to travel. Of course, he traveled on the Yangtze River; this isle was in the Yangtze River, the southern river in China. There are two rivers: in the north the Yellow River, in the south there is this Yangtze River. This isle is in the Yangtze River. He passed by this isle many times and in different seasons. So one Spring he passed by, and as he was taking in the sight, he was so impressed, that he composed a poem, and these two lines,—I would say, this couplet is the highlight of the poem. And this is Li Bai's description of the beauty of Mother Nature. The first two lines are about the beauty of a mortal, a human. But this second couplet that I chose is a description of Mother Nature. So even though the isle has since been sunk, yet these two lines, as long as there is Chinese language, these two lines will prevail (see **Figure 2**).

yān kāi lán yè xiāmng fǎng nuǎn
(smoke/mist open orchid leaf fragrant warm wind)
àn jiā táo huām jǐn làng sheng
(riverbank pressed-between-peach blossom colorful brocade wave birth)

The first character is "smoke," "mist," or "fog." Obviously, it's Springtime, warm weather, and it's mixed with cold weather, early Spring; *yan kai*, the mist, is split, is opening, dispersing. Third character is orchid. Forgive me for not teaching you the beautiful etymology because of the time. The fourth character, you might have thought that orchid would be followed by "blossom" because that third character only refers to the species of the flower. It doesn't mean the opening flowery blossom. So usually it's *lán* followed by *hua*. But surprisingly, Li Bai being Li Bai, he would not be so common or so regular, so he has to do something different. So the line "orchid leaves," the *leaves* of an orchid, meaning he is giving the reader, he providing some literary, poetic mystery—he doesn't tell you the flowers. He saves it. Let's see what he does.

So the mist, the fog is lifting, and the fog does not open up anything, but the fog is so dense, sure looks like it's hiding the orchid leaves. But the fact is, when the fog, when the mist is touching the leaves, automatically the fog opens up. But here, this second character *kai* can be a transitive verb that means "to open up," "to disperse." So the abstract is doing something to something of the substance of the real object, which is orchid leaves, and that is already the magic versus realism—the first four characters.

The fifth character is "fragrant"; for this character I will teach you the etymology. There are two components. The top component is grain—rice or wheat, or sorghum, any grain. Does it look a little bit like a plant, like a tree, the top part of the fifth character *xiang*, and the translation is "fragrant." Look at the Chinese character: The top is grain, the bottom is the Sun. The grain is basking in the Sun, and when the ancient Chinese farmer is walking past the rice field or wheat field, and he smells the grain is growing, and what does he smell? Mmm! Fragrance. Not Chanel No. 9. [laughter] To the ancient Chinese, fragrance is when the grain is in the Sun. That is the Chinese character for "fragrant" or "fragrance."

And the sixth character is "wind," as we studied it before, *fēng* is "wind." And the last character is "warm."

So the first line reads, "The mist or the fog has opened up and you see the orchid leaves and the fragrant breeze is so warm." Of course, it is a Spring day. But it doesn't say "the orchid blossoms are fragrant," although orchid blossoms are very fragrant—they have a special, intoxicating fragrance.

In the second line,— this poem is not written in the style of a ballad. It's written in the style of pentasyllabic, regulated verse. So the total scheme is extremely

important, but I wish I had more time so I could talk in detail about the total scheme. But to put it very simply: The two lines must be arranged like this. The part of speech of the parallel characters must ideally be the opposite, antithetical. But if they are parallel, it's okay too. But at least they have to be related, whether it's antithetic or parallel. But the tone of the matching characters must be the opposite, meaning the line, say, is bb aa bb a; second line must be aa bb aa b. So, high-high low-low high-high low; matched by, low-low high-high low-low high. So both in picture and in music, it's *yin* and *yang*—if the two forces are perfect, then life is perfect. There is this perfect balance between the two forces.

So the first character is a noun, and it's abstract; it's some object that's not tangible—it's intangible, it's mist—*yān* and smoke goes up, so the sound is first a high tone—*yān*. *Kāi* is "open," so we have high tone and high tone. And then you have *lán*, "orchid," is again high. But in the first and the third character there is an exception to the rule. They can be the same as the first and the third in the second line; that's allowed. Otherwise, it's too, too difficult to compose a poem. Because a poem, this art form, is very, very contrived, man-made, after a lot of thinking and arrangement. But ultimately, the lines must look very natural. So that is art.

So the first character of the second line is nothing intangible, because it means "riverbank." So one is "smoke," one is "riverbank," which is soil basically, it's earth versus "mist," which is abstract and intangible. And the second character—what's amazing is that the second character of the first line, *kāi*, is "open," and the picture is a door. And then you see the bolt on the door—you remove the bolt and the door can be opened. And the second character of the second line is what? Putting two things underneath your arms and pressing them between the flesh very closely, tightly, so it doesn't fall down. So one is open, one is pressed against each other. Do you see the two verbs being so different? In the first line, the second character is *kāi*; and the second character of the second line is *jiām*, it's low. So the *yang* and *yin*, the masculine force is matched by a character of feminine force, *àn jia*.

What does it mean that riverbanks are pressing against each other? Let's study the following, then I will explain.

And the third character of the second line is

"peach" which is the match of "orchid" of the third character of the first line. Are you with me so far? Because this is the highest literary genre in Classical Chinese. So to explain this, it takes a little concentration. I hope I make myself very clear. Good, I'm so glad.

So the third character is "peach," just the generic word for peach tree; it doesn't necessarily mean peach blossom at all; but the fourth character is *huā*—it's flower blossom, therefore peach blossom. So the match to "orchid leaf" is "peach blossom." Do you see that? So peach blossoms would emanate a most intoxicating fragrance, much richer, much more intoxicating than the subtle fragrance of the orchid blossoms.

So the peach blossoms are blooming. How do we know they are blooming? The following character, the fifth character tells you. The fifth character is a colorful brocade, and brocade is made of silk, or of gold, or something beautiful already. This character is brocade, but colorful and with multi-colors. And the sixth character is "waves," because if you have riverbanks obviously they're by the river, and on the river what is there? Water. The waves are moving, but the waves are in brocade colors, more gorgeous, more multi-colored, which is of course the reflections of the peach blossoms. Are you with me? So you know what that is that smells so good. That's why in the first line he only introduces the orchid *leaves*, because it's early Spring, and the orchid does not open up until late Summer, or most of the time, early Autumn. So actually it is the peach blossoms which are in full bloom and that turn the waves into something even more colorful, a gorgeous brocade. And the waves are generated, they are flowing—why? Because when the waters see the flowers so beautiful and so fragrant, they come out to see what's going on, and thus, waves are created.

So that's the second line, and that's the beauty of Mother Nature.

So the two lines: The last character of the first line is "warm," and of the second line is "be born, birth," or "generate." So nothing can be born from coldness. As T.S. Eliot wisely pointed out in his "Waste Land" in the first line: "April is the cruellest month..." because of the dead soil, the Earth, and the life of plants trying to struggle out of the Earth's soil, as it is beginning to get a little warmer. So it is with warmth that something grows. So this is the line. And the fragrant wind in the first line is matched beautifully by the "brocade-like waves." Do you see the matching game? And the sound goes like this [recites]. So you see, the first one ends *nuǎn* and the second line ends with *sheng*, which is usually how a Tang dynasty poem will end—however wistful and sad the poem might be, yet the tone at the end will always save the day. The tone of the last character must always be either rising or high to save the day.

Now, I'll read it one more time. [recites] So that's how it goes.

Literati Painting

Li Bai had to wait almost 700 years for another great master to emerge, in poetry, calligraphy, and painting, all of them, and together when the three genres were all matured, they came to a beautiful union, and it becomes another cultural genre, only limited, strictly limited to Chinese culture, which is called *wenrenhua*, or literati painting.

And about this painter, quickly—Shi Tao is his name. He's also a calligrapher and painter. He's from 1643-1707, you see, almost 700 years after Li Bai.

By the time Shi Tao emerged, the Parrot Isle had long gone, had long sunk into the Yangtze River. But from these two poetic lines, because Shi Tao loved—well, the only similarity between the unwitty me, and this great Shi Tao, is our mutual love, of or for Li Bai. But then, almost all Chinese people love Li Bai.

Social phenomena and political phenomena can have their day, but culture and poetry last forever. So if you come across a Chinese friend who says he or she doesn't even know Li Bai, quickly wave them goodbye, never to see them again! [laughter]

About Shi Tao, one of the towering artists of literati painting—which is a unique genre blending poetry, calligraphy, and painting—Shi Tao was a descendant of the founding emperor of the Ming dynasty. A great admirer of Li Bai, Shi Tao fashioned this work of art out of a couplet from a heptasyllabic, regulated verse (with eight lines) by the master poet, which glows in its poetic splendor as it is ablaze with color and spirit, and which has exerted tremendous influence on later artists of the genre (see next page).

So if you see this painting, which is beautifully designed, he has imagined Parrot Isle, because by the time he was born, the island had long gone. But from the poet, he gathered from his imagination,—I think

Literati painting by Shi Tao.

two lines, in a special calligraphic style, which is called "clerical calligraphic style," usually practiced to put down official governmental documents in ancient times. Shi Tao was good at all four major calligraphic styles. So I would, if I were the painter, I would definitely set this painting into a free style with a bravura spirit, which is called "running" or "cursive" style. But not our great master. He deliberately put down "clerical" style to match this, because he is saying this is great, there is poetic merit. And the cursive style calligraphy, or running calligraphic style will only belittle these two great lines.

And also the way he executed this clerical style—his clerical style is not dry or pedantic: The characters come to light; they are beautiful. So those are the two lines. And someone asked me about the color, and the smaller characters. It says, "this is from Li Bai's poem 'Parrot Isle,'" and then he signed his own literary sobriquet.

Now, this is a very short talk, but I really hope … I mean, you know in exactly two weeks it will be Chinese New Year, and we call it the Spring Festival, because we feel it is the season which functions as a harbinger of the coming Spring, and so we call it the Spring Festival. So the prospect of the coming Spring in this merciless, cold season—we're anticipating the Spring to come.

human imagination can do a lot, and this is beautiful. Not only the color. Now colors rarely appear in Classical Chinese paintings. The Chinese people believe ink can open up to ten shades of colors. We don't need color. But in this case, he must, because there are two poetic lines, they are ablaze with colors, so he painted this.

And he saved—the other side is the Blue Mountain—and on the other side, the top right, these are the

So the prospect of Spring and the talk of this eternal beauty of Chinese Classical poetry—is almost like a dual blessing. It's a dual blessing which can lift ourselves and which can give special distinction to our existence. So if my small talk, my brief talk can enhance your interest in Classical Chinese poetry, or Chinese culture, or poetry, in general, however little there is, I will not have come in vain.

Thank you so much. [applause]

'STRENGTH TO LOVE'

A Special Tribute to Dr. King

by Dennis Speed

Justice, truthfulness, and those creative powers by means of which we may discover valid, revolutionary principles of our universe, form a seamless whole, in which Classical culture, morality, and physical science are united by a common passion for universal justice and truth. *Where are the men and women fit to lead us in the pathway toward safety, the pathway toward rule by the principles of truth and justice, not 'popular opinion'?*

—Lyndon LaRouche
"The Substance of Morality," 1998

Jan. 24—**"Strength To Love": A Unity Concert—A special tribute in honor of Dr. Martin Luther King Jr.'s vision of the future,** was the name of the flagship

event which culminated a two-day "congress" held by the Schiller Institute, in collaboration with The Foundation for the Revival of Classical Culture.

A combination of Italian operatic arias by composer Giuseppe Verdi, German songs by Franz Schubert and J.S. Bach, and African-American Spirituals, set both for chorus and for single voice, made up the concert repertoire.

The 350 concert participants were also presented with the cantata for voice and piano, *The Life of Christ*, composed in 1948 by the renowned tenor, Roland Hayes. It consists of ten core selections, with other additional songs capable of being added, according to the performer's wishes.

For this particular occasion, there was an ensemble of three voices—soloist tenors Everett Suttle and Regi-

EIRNS/Robert Wesser

The Schiller Institute NY Community Chorus and guest soloists at the Martin Luther King, Jr., Unity Concert, Co-Cathedral of St. Joseph, Brooklyn, Jan. 15.

nald Bouknight, and baritone Frank Mathis—who chose to add four songs to the core of ten. A fourth voice, that of Roland Hayes as narrator, was supplied by mezzo Elvira Green. The quartet was accompanied at the piano by Gregory Hopkins, singer, organist, conductor, and Artistic Director for the Harlem Opera Theater.

Both Green and Hopkins worked for decades with renowned vocal coach Sylvia Olden Lee, the first African-American ever hired by the Metropolitan Opera in New York City. Lee was a member of the Schiller Institute Advisory Board for nearly ten years, until her passing in 2004.

Such a performance of

Roland Hayes' cantata, The Life of Christ, *was performed by three voices supported by piano and narrator. From left, Gregory Hopkins (piano), Everett Suttle (tenor), Reginald Bouknight (tenor), Frank Mathis (baritone), and Elvira Green (narrator).*

The Life of Christ has rarely occurred, if ever at all. This presentation of the piece was intended to emphasize the dramatic content of Hayes' narrative of the Christ story, as well as the reverent simplicity of his settings. Hayes consciously wished to invoke the mood, and approximate the form, of Bach's weekly cantata offerings that he wrote as new compositions for his church at Leipzig. The effect of the multiply-connected voicing of the performing quintet was to focus the audience on the arc of the piece, rather than the particular song being performed.

Monsignor Kieran Harrington—the Co-Cathedral of St. Joseph at which he serves televised the entire concert live—had introduced the entirety with an invocation, prior to which he gave brief remarks of welcome. He stressed the role that such events, dedicated to the theme of unity, could have in internationalizing the vision of the United States, to take into consideration conditions of war and crisis worldwide. He named the nations of Syria, Nigeria, and Venezuela, where war, terrorism and economic catastrophe are a fact of daily life.

By "unity" is meant not the infantile "why can't we all just get along?" but the unity of the American repub-

lic, as Alexander Hamilton and Gouverneur Morris, Hamilton's closest friend, had stated that principle of unity in the Preamble of the Constitution of the United States, which Morris drafted.

Monsignor Harrington then introduced the New York Police Department Ceremonial Unit, including William Bove, bass-baritone, to sing "God Bless America."

Later, Schiller Institute spokesman Dennis Speed revealed to the audience that "God Bless America" was being performed in honor of the Alexandrov Ensemble, 64 of whose members were killed on Christmas Day 2016 in a plane crash. The Alexandrov Ensemble had performed "God Bless America" to honor the United States and the New York City Police Department on the tenth anniversary of September 11. The NYPD Ceremonial Unit, led by Lt. Tony Giorgio, had just joined the Schiller Institute in conducting an outdoor commemorative ceremony at the Teardrop Memorial in Bayonne, New Jersey, on Orthodox Christmas Day, Saturday, Jan. 7, 2017.

In one sense, *each* musical offering in the concert was in the form of a prayer. Many of the audience were aware that this year, 2017, marks the 50th anniversary of King's famous speech against the Vietnam War, delivered at New York City's Riverside Church on April 4, 1967. King momentarily, back then, almost lost everything because he gave that speech. Newspapers, including the *New York Times*, denounced him. Contributions dried up. His popularity sank to an all-time low.

Already affected by the diminution of his influence among African-American youth as a result of the Black Power slogan and movement of 1967-68, and by internal criticism of his "splitting his attention" between his controversial Vietnam War stand and his defense of striking sanitation workers in Memphis, Tennessee—when King gave his final speech on April 3, 1968, he was not the popular Nobel Peace Prize-winner of December 1964. "He was despised and rejected" by his former liberal-establishment backers.

The selections, Schubert's *Ave Maria* and Bach's *Bist du bei mir,* respectively performed by sopranos Indira Mahajan and Gudrun Buhler, were not only chosen for their relative familiarity. They are both prayers of persons contemplating death. "Abide with me, and I shall go joyfully to my death and to my peace," says the singer in the Bach work. Indira Mahajan's *Ave Maria* performance of the familiar Catholic prayer, in the Latin rarely heard today in the Catholic Church, was particularly noted and appreciated.

The Verdi operatic selections that followed, taken from his *Don Carlos,* originally written by Germany's greatest playwright Friedrich Schiller, and from Shakespeare's *Othello,* are also prayers. The first is Verdi's *Dio, che nell'alma infondere,* simultaneously a prayer and a freedom song, a duet in which the two singers (Frank Mathis and Everett Suttle) reinforce each other in their mutual commitment to a cause. The second, Desdemona's *Salce! Salce!* (Willow! Willow!) aria, one of the most famous in opera, was so well per-

Tiger Butterfly Films

The concert included arias by Verdi, songs by Schubert and Bach, and African-American Spirituals, set both for chorus and for single voice.

formed by Gudrun Buhler that there was no immediate reaction from the audience—only silence. Desdemona's agony as she awaits her certain execution at the hands of her deeply beloved Othello—a fate she does not deserve and did not cause, but cannot change—does not diminish her love for him.

Gethsemane in Memphis

As with Abraham Lincoln's Gettysburg Address and Second Inaugural Address,—there were two great speeches that defined King's public life in America. His "March on Washington" speech was given in front of over 250,000 people and simultaneously televised. His speech in Memphis, "I've Been to the Mountain-Top," which was essentially extemporized, was given to just over 600 people, in a two-thirds filled church, on a rainy, stormy night, and has been seen or heard, in its entirety, by far fewer people. The conclusion of the speech is well known:

Like anybody, I would like to live a long life. Longevity has its place. But I'm not concerned about that now. I just want to do God's will. And He's allowed me to go up to the mountain. And I've looked over. And I've seen the Promised Land. I may not get there with you. But I want you to know tonight, that we as a people, will get to the Promised Land. And so, I'm happy tonight. So I'm not worried about anything. I'm not fearing any man! Mine eyes have seen the glory of the coming of the Lord.

It is the beginning of the speech that makes it clear that King has imitated Christ, and has consciously placed himself on the stage of universal history. This is not merely a personally-willed decision, but an ontologically willed decision:

Something is happening in Memphis; something is happening in our world. And you know, if I was standing at the beginning of time, with the possibility of taking a kind of general and panoramic view of the whole of human history up to now, and the Almighty said to me, "Martin Luther King, which age would you like to live in?" I would take my mental flight by Egypt, and I would watch God's children in their magnificent trek from the dark dungeons of Egypt through, or rather across the Red Sea, through the wilderness on toward the promised land. And in spite of its significance, I would't stop there.

I would move on by Greece and take my mind to Mount Olympus. And I would see Plato, Aristotle, Socrates, Euripides, and Aristophanes assembled around the Parthenon. And I would watch them around the Parthenon as they discussed the great and eternal issues of reality. But I wouldn't stop there.

I would go on, even to the great heyday of the Roman Empire ... But I wouldn't stop there. I would even come up to the day of the Renaissance, and get a quick picture of all that the Renaissance did for the cultural and aesthetic life of man. But I wouldn't stop there....

Strangely enough, I would turn to the Almighty and say, "If you will allow me to live just a few years in the second half of the twentieth century, I will be happy."

Now that's a strange statement to make, ...

King's speech was not, as most believe, a wild preacher's rhetorical ecstasy at its conclusion, but was a 43-minute, conscious and optimistic acceptance of Gethsemane. It is a magnificent act of courage, like that committed by the historical Jeanne D'Arc, which directly led to the creation of the French nation. King's assassination less than 24 hours later by a multiple-person unit—and not by "lone assassin" James Earl Ray, who later denied being King's executioner and co-wrote a book entitled "Who Killed Martin Luther King?"—was neither unexpected nor sought, but it also was not feared. It was the inner music of his intent to act for the cause of freedom that King relied upon for his power. That power was not singular with King, but was the wellspring of intent that he knew to be contained in the African-American Spiritual. King's ability to invoke this power in his audiences, African-American and otherwise, stemmed from his ability, as Roland Hayes also demonstrated, to hear the divine spark of, not resignation, but optimistic defiance of the slave mentality.

It was in order to bring this re-assessment of King's last hours to life in the minds of the audience that Hayes' *Life of Christ* was selected. Hayes' unique experience of the African-American Spiritual's Classical roots—in the sense in which the Schiller Institute utilizes that term, along with the Foundation for the Revival of Classical Culture—qualifies his portrait of Christ as the perfect frame for rendering with psychological truth "the imitation of Christ" that was King's final hours.

Despite the fact that all who participated wittingly and with forethought in preserving the institution of slavery, turned themselves and every social institution with which they were associated into animals—except the slaves—the preservation of the humanity of the nation was still made possible through the invention of the African-American Spiritual. The performance by the Schiller Institute NYC Chorus, conducted by Diane Sare, Founder and Co-Director of the group, of three Spirituals at the beginning of the program, managed to capture this idea. In particular the Spiritual, "Soon Ah Will Be Done (With the Troubles of the World)," illustrates this. The chorus, which sang at the beginning of the concert, then took its seats, and shifted its choral role to that of audience.

The Schiller Institute intends to increase its "singer audience" to 1,500 people in the coming months, as a way of providing a cultural paradigm-shift to occur in parallel with the "new economic platform" that must needs be brought about in the current circumstance. The very survival of the United States may depend on re-employing the key components of American Classi-

Tiger Butterfly Films

Chorus founder Diane Sare (shown) and music director John Sigerson conducted the chorus.

cal culture, such as the African-American Spiritual as developed, preserved, and performed by Roland Hayes, Sylvia Lee, Hall Johnson, Harry Burleigh, and Antonin Dvorak, to allow today's citizens "to stand on the rock where Moses"—and Dr. Martin Luther King, Jr.—stood.

The Mission of Roland Hayes

Jan. 24—The following are excerpts from Roland Hayes' foreword to his book, My Songs: Aframerican Religious Folk Songs Arranged and Interpreted by Roland Hayes *(1948).*

I was born just twenty-four years after the Emancipation Proclamation. The atmosphere of the slave days was still strong at my place of birth and the religious folk songs of my people were being born out of religious experience at white heat. I have seen them being born in our religious services at the community Mount Zion Baptist Church at "Little Row" (now Curryville), Gordon County, Georgia. Here I heard great ritual sermons preached and prayers prayed, and I sang the Aframerican religious folk songs as a child with my parents and the church folk. Later, I was for four years a music special student at Fisk University in Nashville, Tennessee, and I acquired additions to the knowledge I already had of our folk songs from their pioneer collections.

In London and Paris, where I lived for twelve years, I made my home with some highly intelligent native Africans, most from the West Coast of Africa, who were making university studies under government auspices. Discussions of the music of African peoples in Africa and Aframerican folk music were mutually enlightening. Aframerican folk songs, forgotten since childhood, sprang to my lips, and to my astonishment my native African audience joined in the music while expressing what they felt in their own language idiom. This pointed out to me the African characteristics in Aframerican folk songs, and in the heat of discovery the dross was separated from pure metal, to borrow a figure from the iron foundry in Chattanooga where I worked as a youth.

Eventually, I obtained recordings of African music, and a collection of musical instruments used in them, which I learned to manipulate well enough to understand them. From my African friends in London, and later from African visitors to my home, I learned how instrumental effects are sometimes implied in the vocal characteristics of the older Aframerican folk songs. These and other studies I have drawn upon in some of my accompaniments.

The term "Negro" is a misnomer when taken to mean that in anything but color the slaves within the borders of the various Southern states, or the various plantations—or even anywhere—were of one universal type. But for those Africans who were transplanted to the United States the term "Aframerican" seems fitting.

In the same work, he began his introduction to his Life of Christ *cycle as follows.*

The salvation of man is always the great theme of masterworks in literature and art. Biblical material follows like a red thread in mankind's art works through the ages. No story appeals to man's finer creative vision as does the life of Christ. The early Christian chants, the masses of Palestrina, the passions, oratorios, masses of Bach, Handel, Beethoven—among many others—are the musical panorama of the mute majesty of the life of God on earth. With never diminishing radiance, to every succeeding generation of humanity this panorama gives life, spiritual consciousness, to each in his own measures. It is small wonder that in his turn the Aframerican should find in his musical portraying of the life of Christ, his most effective utterance. A social condition of the most abject humility could not help but find complete identity in a life of love, compassion, and patience.

'Unity Concert' Program

The Tablet, *the newspaper of the Brooklyn Diocese of the Roman Catholic Church, published the following notice on Jan. 11, under the title, "Co-Cathedral to Host Unity Concert Honoring Dr. King."*

The Foundation for the Revival of Classical Culture and the Schiller Institute will conduct a "Unity Concert" entitled "Strength to Love" to commemorate the birthday of the Rev. Martin Luther King Jr., Jan. 15, at 4 p.m. at St. Joseph's Co-Cathedral, Prospect Heights.

"In this time of division in our country, a certain trumpet for unity should be sounded. The language of music is an excellent way to sound that trumpet," said Lynne Speed, of The Schiller Institute.

The concert will feature the "Life of Christ" song cycle composed by Roland Hayes. The program will also include a soloist from the NYPD Ceremonial Unit singing "God Bless America," three African American spirituals and the "Amen" Chorus from Handel's *Messiah* (Dr. King's favorite piece), performed by the Schiller Institute NY Community Chorus.

Guest soloists will perform selections from works of Schubert, Bach and Verdi. Special guest artists include: Indira Mahajan, Everett Suttle, Reginald Bouknight, Frank Mathis, Gudrun Buhler, Elvira Green, and

Gregory Hopkins. Conductors are Diane Sare and John Sigerson, who conducted the historic Mozart *Requiem* at the Co-Cathedral of St. Joseph on the 15th anniversary commemoration of 9-11.

Music has long been at the center of the African-American struggle for freedom in the 17th- and 18th-century American colonies, as well as in the later United States. "Freedom songs" were not merely composed by African-Americans confined in slavery, but also by free churchmen associated with the African Methodist Episcopal Church and the African Methodist Episcopal Zion Church.

Even before the founding of those churches in 1794 and 1821, respectively, African-American clergymen heading churches in Florida, Virginia, South Carolina, and elsewhere composed songs. Literacy training existed, including of slaves, as early as 1634 in Quebec, carried out by Jesuit instructors such as Paul Le Jeanne, and the 1640s in Pennsylvania, carried out by the Moravians. The use in the 1960s civil rights movement of "freedom songs" was a central weapon employed to "overcome them with our capacity to love," as King once stated.

"Public service through public action" was the most enduring lesson of Dr. King. Among his early associates, nearly all of whom were clergymen, there had been a debate—"Why are you always talking about the 'Social' gospel," and not the 'Gospel' gospel?" King was often criticized by other clergymen and church institutions.

When he was denounced as "an outside agitator" in Birmingham, Ala., in April of 1963, King, then incarcerated at Birmingham jail, responded, "I am in Birmingham because injustice is here. Just as the prophets of the eighth century B.C. left their villages and carried their 'thus saith the Lord' far beyond the boundaries of their home towns, and just as the Apostle Paul left his village of Tarsus and carried the gospel of Jesus Christ to the far corners of the Greco-Roman world, so am I compelled to carry the gospel of freedom beyond my own home town. Like Paul, I must constantly respond to the Macedonian call for aid."

It is often forgotten that the King-associated civil rights movement was not a political movement. It was a religiously based crusade for human dignity and justice that was punctuated by non-violent direct action.

IV. From Lyndon LaRouche's Prison Writings

LaRouche was framed up by George H.W. Bush, and falsely imprisoned for five years, 1989-94.

Mozart's 1782-1786 Revolution In Music

by Lyndon H. LaRouche, Jr.

July, 1992

This lengthy study is one of many written by Lyndon LaRouche while he was incarcerated. It was originally published in **Fidelio** *magazine, Winter 1992.*

I.

Contrary to widespread, illiterate custom, the word "Classical," when employed in its strictest, epistemological sense, signifies any species of fine-arts composition which coheres with Plato's principles for aesthetics.[1] More recently, all of the development of modern Classical polyphony, from Florence, Italy of the early Fifteenth Century, through the 1896 Johannes Brahms' composing his "Four Serious Songs," defines—as we have noted elsewhere—a corresponding phase of musical progress to be of a specific *Cantor Type.*[2] In this following review of a forthcoming musical textbook,[3] we shall focus upon a still narrower interval of time, the crowning accomplishment in all musical development to date, that century-odd development of Classical polyphony which began with Joseph Haydn's revolutionary six "Russian" string quartets, Opus 33, of 1781. We concentrate here upon a crucial facet of that three-fold, Haydn-Mozart musical revolution of 1781-1786, which began the ensuing hundred-odd years of progress.

This revolution of 1781-1786 combines three distinct revolutions into one. Each of these three is defined as a "revolution" in its own right, in the same sense we

Wolfgang Amadeus Mozart

attribute that quality to a valid discovery of principle in physical science.[4] Taken in order of their impact upon Wolfgang Amadeus Mozart, these three revolutions are as follows. The first in this sequence, is Haydn's discovery of his *Motivführung* principle of composition, as this is represented by his 1781, Opus 33 string quartets.[5] The

1. Lyndon H. LaRouche, Jr., "The Classical Idea: Natural and Artistic Beauty," *Fidelio,* Vol. I, No. 2, Spring 1992.

2. Lyndon H. LaRouche, Jr., "On the Subject of Metaphor," *Fidelio,* Vol. I, No. 3, Fall 1992.

3. *A Manual on the Rudiments of Tuning and Registration,* Vol. I, Schiller Institute, Washington, D.C., pp. 229-260.

4. LaRouche, "Metaphor," *op. cit.*

5. Joseph Haydn, *String Quartets Opus 20 and 33, Complete Edition,* ed. by Wilhelm Altmann (New York: Dover Publications, 1985). For a discussion of the influence of Haydn's Motivführung principle on Mozart's compositional method, see Hermann Abert, *W.A. Mozart, neu-*

second, is Johann Sebastian Bach's 1747 *Musical Offering.*[6] The third, is Mozart's insight into the integration of these two preceding discoveries by Haydn and Bach. Mozart's discovery is represented immediately by a series of his compositions from the 1782-1786 interval. Among the most notable of these latter, are his six "Haydn" string quartets (K. 387, 421, 428, 458, 464, 465), his C-minor Mass (K. 427), his keyboard fantasy-sonata (K. 475/457), and his celebrated keyboard concerti in D-minor (K. 466) and C-minor (K. 491).

The characteristic feature of this 1781-1782 Haydn-Mozart revolution, is the successful development of a principled new conceptual approach to Classical composition, an approach by means of which a complete work—such as a theme with variations and fugue, or a sonata, or a symphony, or a concerto, or a string quartet—might achieve that singular perfection of unity of effect which is the subject of Plato's **Parmenides** dialogue, the dialogue on the matter of "the One and the Many."[7] The subject of this following review is a crucial aspect of that three-fold revolution of 1781-1786, the relation of those discoveries to the principle of "Platonic ideas." That aspect is identified by the term "musical thought-object."

That Haydn-Bach-Mozart revolution is the underlying, unifying theme of the forthcoming, second volume of a two-volume musical textbook, *A Manual on the Rudiments of Tuning and Registration.*[8] Volume I, a Fall 1992 release, covers, principally, tuning and the registration of the *bel canto*-trained species of polyphonic singing voices. The second volume, for 1993 release, treats the circa 1815-1849 perfection of the Classical chest of orchestral and keyboard instruments,[9] from the standpoint of *bel canto* vocal polyphony. This second volume uses Beethoven's integration of soloist, chorus, and orchestra in his *Missa Solemnis* and *Ninth Symphony* as benchmarks for portraying the overall development of

the Classical performing medium during the period from Handel and Bach through Brahms' work.

Once the 1781-1786 *Motivführung* revolution had been established, by Haydn, Mozart, and then Beethoven, the polyphonic medium of performance must be brought into conformity, in form and application, with the requirements of that new principle of composition. The pivotal instrumental feature of the required congruence, is the evolved string quartet of Haydn, Mozart, Beethoven, *et al.*: two violins, viola, and 'cello. This combination is a musical medium in its own right, but also the kernel of the Classical chest of orchestral instruments.

To make this connection clearer to the non-professional: each species of *bel canto* singing voice (soprano, mezzo-soprano, contralto, tenor, baritone, bass) is distinguished from the others by its own, unique, spectroscopic set of register-passing frequency-bands (see **Figure 1**). Each string of each species of string instrument is an available surrogate for some individual register of a species of singing voice (see **Figure 2**). Thus, if a composer assigns the part of a soprano voice to the first violin, a mezzo-soprano to the second violin, a tenor to the viola, and a bass to the 'cello, the performer need but pass to a different register (string) on the appropriate choice of register-passing tone (see **Table I**).

However—to continue to the next step of this illustration—by changing the register-passages of an instrument in the relevant fashion, the performer can imitate the registral spectroscopy of any species of singing voice—although, often, in a vocal range displaced from that of the singer (see **Figure 3**). In contrast to this facility of the strings, wind instruments (see **Figure 4**) have essentially fixed registral characteristics, each corresponding to a specific choice of singing-voice species. Thus, the use of the polyphonic principle perfected by Handel, Bach, Haydn, Mozart, *et al.*, implicitly requires greater emphasis upon the highly developed form of string ensemble, centered upon the string quartet, as the keystone of the Classical orchestra. The Haydn *Motivführung* principle, as apprehended by Mozart, takes us to the heart of this challenge for development of the appropriate approach to composition for the orchestra.

Consider an illustration of this point from Mozart's 1782 C-minor Mass, K. 427 (see **Box,** page 50). The violin here is imitating the soprano singing voice, but at a displaced range. The point is illustrated in another respect, by studying cases of Mozart's and Beethoven's transcriptions for strings of some of their own earlier

bearbeitete und erweiterte Ausgabe von Otto Jahns Mozart (Leipzig: VEB Breitkopf und Härtel, 1983), Vol. II, pp. 135-151.

6. J.S. Bach, *Musikalisches Opfer-Musical Offering-Offrance musicale,* ed. by Carl Czerny (New York: Edition Peters, No. 219).

7. Lyndon H. LaRouche, Jr., "Solution to Plato's Paradox: The 'One' and the 'Many'," **Fidelio**, Vol. I, No. 1, Winter 1991, *passim.*

8. See footnote 3.

9. The Lord Palmerston-linked "Young Europe" insurrection of 1848-1849 coincided with an assault upon Beethoven and Classical polyphony generally by such bomb-throwing anarchists as Richard Wagner and his accomplice Bakunin. Part of this assault upon Classical culture was an effort to eliminate an orchestral tuning of C=256 cycles, by aid of redesigning wind instruments to fit the elevated pitch of A=440 or higher.

compositions for wind instruments.[10] The string quartet, augmented by the double bass, generates an orchestral chest of stringed instruments which maps superdensely the entire vocal polyphonic range, and freely extends it for every species of actual or imaginable spectroscopic species of singing voice. The relationship between these stringed choruses and the soloist-like wind instruments, is the key to the evolution of the orchestra, especially from 1781-1782 onward, an orchestra suited to the implied requirements and potentialities of the *Motivführung* revolution.

The Root of the *Motivführung*

In a general way, any person steeped in the Classical polyphonic repertoire should recognize, as if by reflex, many among the leading musical points considered in this review. Even if such a person did not know the crucial circumstances of Haydn's revolutionary Opus 33, certain relevant points are abundantly clear to the same effect from simple observation. The person should be aware of a certain kind of superiority of coherence appearing more and more in the later string quartets, sonatas, symphonies, and concerti of Joseph Haydn, and those of Mozart, both in comparison with the relevant work of the Scarlattis, Handel, Bach, and Bach's famous sons. There is visible to that same effect, a striking, revolutionary change toward much greater coherence, in Haydn's composition, beginning his Opus 33. A study of Haydn's own work of the 1763-1782 interval, and

---

10. To cite just three examples: (a) In 1787, Mozart reworked his Serenade No. 12 in C-minor for 2 Horns, 2 Oboes, 2 Clarinets, and 2 Bassoons, K. 388 (1782), as his Quintet in C-minor, for 2 Violins, 2 Violas, and Violoncello, K. 406. (b) In 1797, Beethoven reworked his Partita in E-flat for Wind Octet, Op. 103 (1792, published posthumously), as his Quintet for 2 Violins, 2 Violas, and Violoncello, Op. 4. (c) In 1801, the firm Mollo published Beethoven's Quintet in E-flat for Pianoforte and Wind Instruments, Op. 16, which he had composed in 1797, and simultaneously published Beethoven's own arrangement of the work as a Quartet for Pianoforte and Strings (not to be confused with a subsequently published arrangement for string quartet alone, which the composer had nothing to do with).

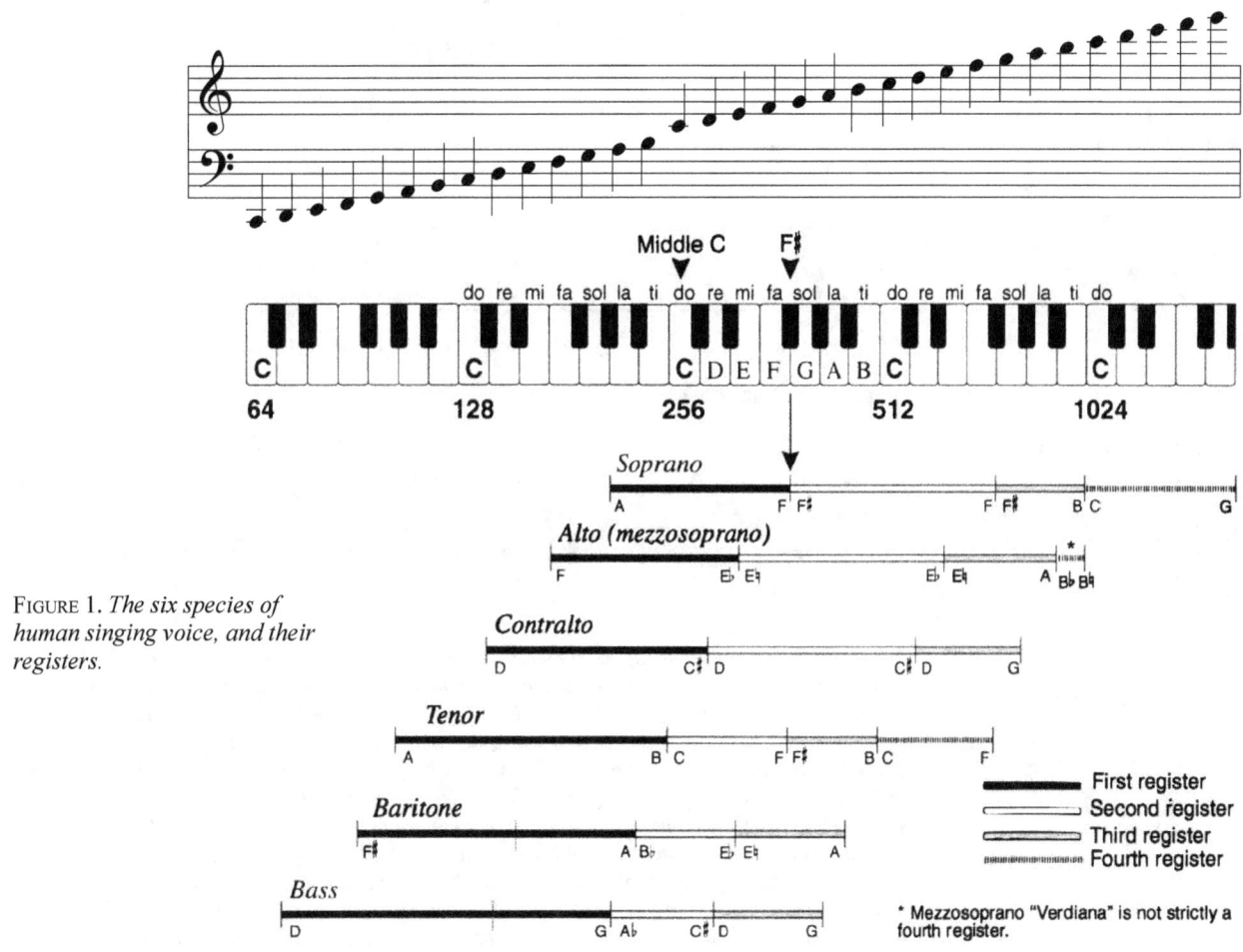

FIGURE 1. *The six species of human singing voice, and their registers.*

also a comparative study of Mozart's work over the 1773-1786 interval, brings the point into clearer focus.

One of the contributing scholars for Volume II of *A Manual on the Rudiments of Tuning and Registration* suggested the following special studies be included. In addition to the obvious comparison of Haydn's Opus 33 with his 1771 Opus 20, "Sun" quartets, compare his 1771/73 Symphony No. 52 with the 1782, more "Bachian" Symphony No. 78. Look back to the Fourth Movement of his 1765 Symphony No. 13; compare this not only with his Symphonies Nos. 52 and 78, but with the Finale of Mozart's 1787 ("Jupiter") Symphony No. 41.

Such comparisons show a persisting, developing effort, in the pre-1781 compositions, to master a stub-born paradox. Suddenly, with the Opus 33, the discovery, the solution bursts into view, as is the case for a valid major discovery in physical science. This Haydn discovery leads Mozart to recognize the special import of an earlier discovery, the *Musical Offering,* by Bach, with the resulting general consequence identified. This process has an eerie resemblance to the most crucial discovery of the Golden Renaissance's founding of modern physical science: Nicolaus of Cusa's discovery of his own "isoperimetric" solution[11] for Archimedes'

---

11. Cardinal Nicolaus of Cusa, *De Docta Ignorantia* (On Learned Ignorance), trans. by Jasper Hopkins as *Nicholas of Cusa on Learned Ignorance* (Minneapolis: Arthur M. Banning Press, 1985), pp. 53-77; see also, "De Circuli Quadratura" ("On the Quadrature of the Circle"), trans. into German by Jay Hoffman (Mainz: Felix Meiner Verlag), *passim.*

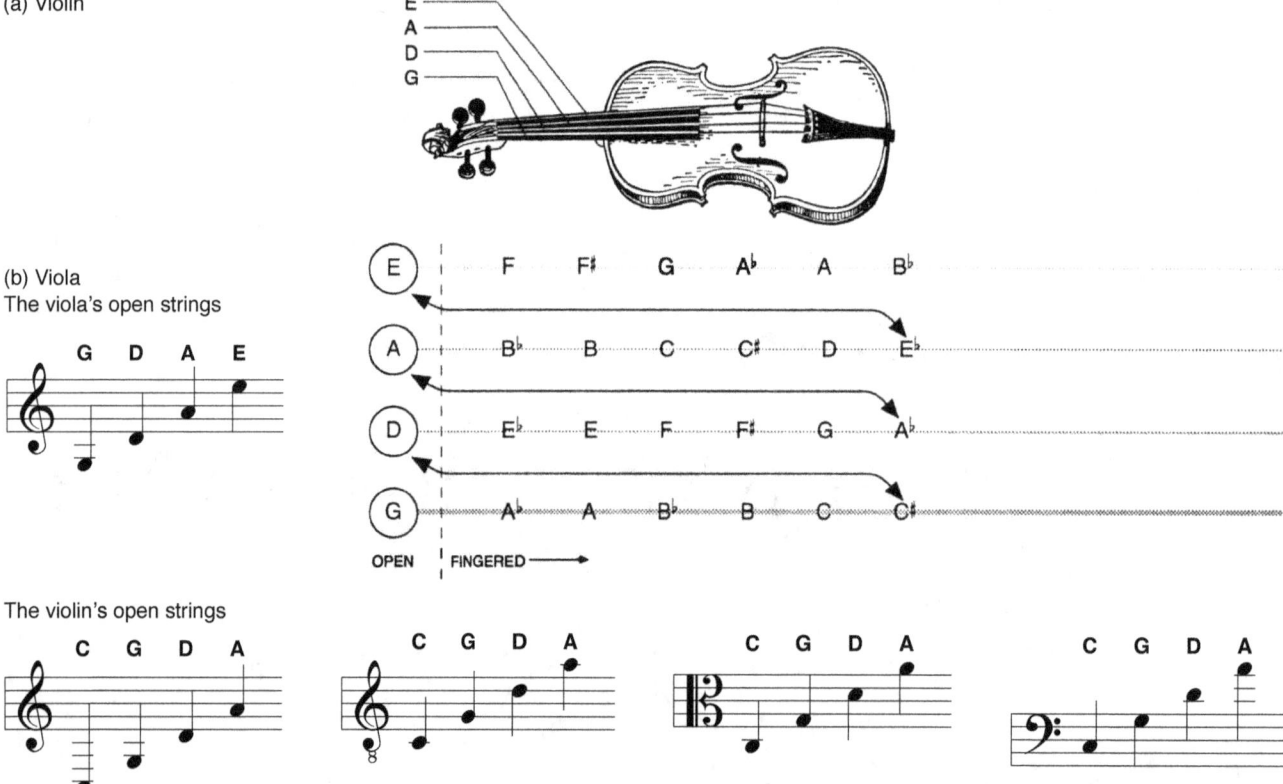

FIGURE 2. *The violin family of instruments was developed in order to imitate, and then extend, the principles of the bel canto singing voice. Each member of the violin family has four strings, with each string tuned at the musical interval of a fifth above or below the adjacent string or strings. (a) In the simplest case, each open (unfingered) string of the violin can be used as the lowest tone of a new surrogate "vocal" register. The succeeding higher tones fingered on that string remain in the same "register," until the player changes to the next-higher string. For example, a register shift is simulated by moving from the C♯ played on the G string, up to the open D string—simulating, for instance, the contralto's shift from first to second register. (b) The same principle applies to the open strings of the viola—C, G, D, and A. Because the viola's range straddles the usual treble and bass clefs, for clarity the same four strings are shown here using four different clefs: the treble clef, the modern tenor clef (sounds one octave lower than the treble clef), the alto clef (in which most viola music is written), and the bass clef. (c) The violoncello's open strings.*

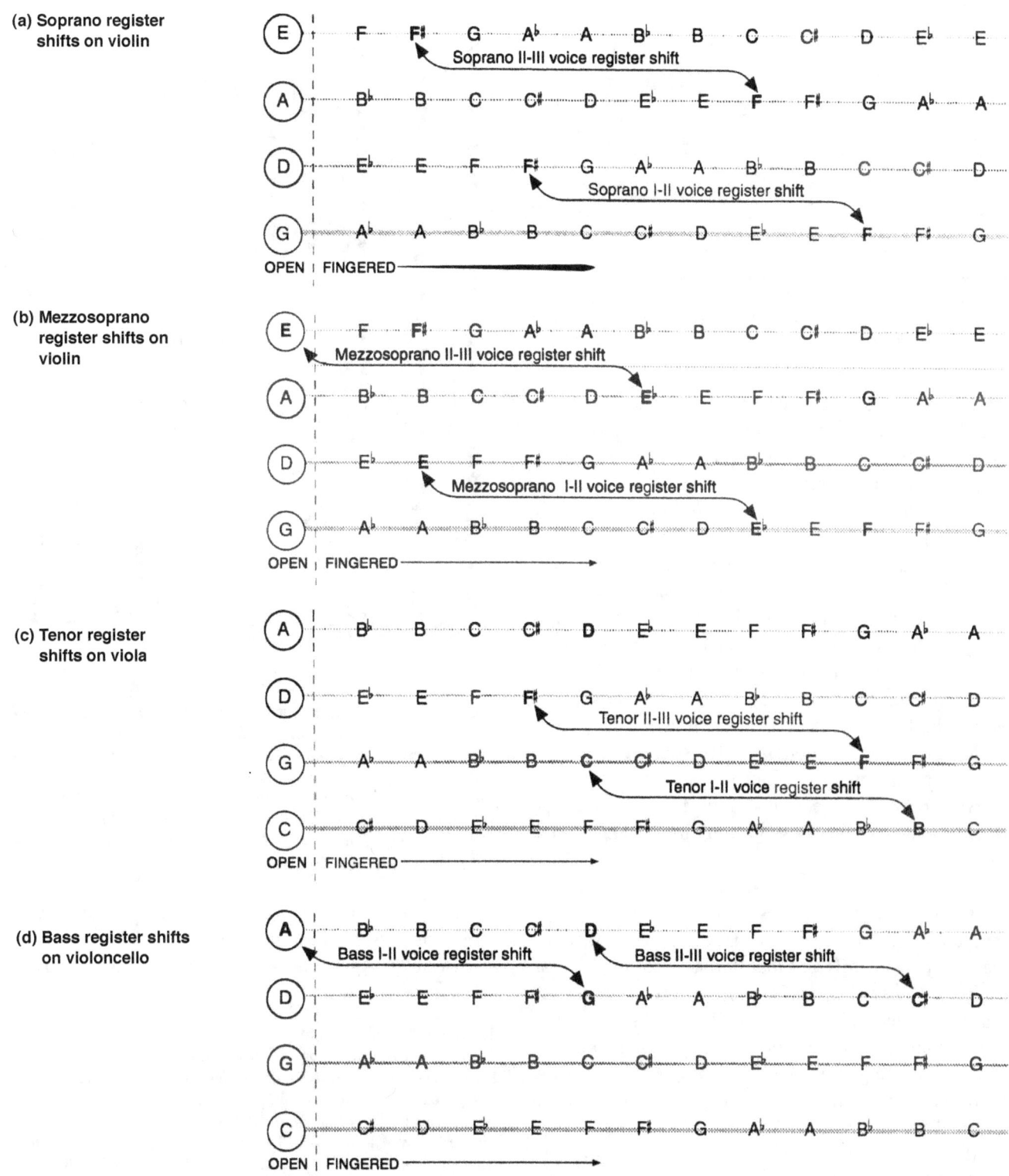

(a) Soprano register shifts on violin

(b) Mezzosoprano register shifts on violin

(c) Tenor register shifts on viola

(d) Bass register shifts on violoncello

TABLE 1. *Each member of the violin family can be fingered in such a way that it can imitate the register shifts of any voice singing within that instrument's range. Here, the violin is shown imitating (a) the soprano, and (b) the mezzosoprano vocal register shifts. For example, the soprano's I-II register shift is imitated by shifting from a fingered F on the G string, to a fingered F♯ on the next-higher D string. The viola is shown imitating the tenor voice species, and the violoncello ('cello) the bass voice. Because these shifts can be made in various places, there are many other possible imitations; also, the four "benchmark" examples shown here are not necessarily the most frequently used. The reader is encouraged to find other possible imitations.*

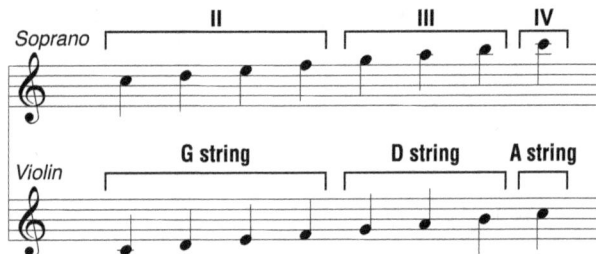

FIGURE 3. *The violin plays the passage sung by the soprano, but at a displacement one octave lower. The octave displacement enables the violinist to imitate the II-III register shift by changing from the G string to the D string, and then the III-IV shift by switching to the A string.*

profoundly paradoxical efforts to define a square whose area is equal to that of a given circle.[12] There is a connection between Cusa's discovery and the *Motivführung* revolution, such that mastering the relevant feature of the former leads us to recognize the most crucial feature of the latter.

Classical music is a form of language, derived from the polyphonic vocalization of Classical forms (e.g., Sanskrit) of poetry. To the degree the vocalization follows the physiologically natural pathway of Florentine *bel canto* voice-training, to a well-tempered polyphony centered upon the C=256 cycles of the child soprano voice, the formal rudiments of the musical language's philology are properly situated for study. The crucial issue then confronts us: "If music is a form of language, to what class of objects does this form of language refer? What is the proper subject of this language called 'music'?"

The subject of Classical polyphony is not the sensuous (e.g., "erotic") features of the musical-language medium (e.g., not "overtones"), but, rather, a different class of object, different than the musical medium as such. To argue to the contrary effect, is as if to propose that the subject of the mathematics professor's classroom oration, is to cause pleasurable sensations in the student's hearing apparatus, or to propose that, for the famished person, the primary object of eating is to amuse the taste-buds.

It is a fair summary, to say that music, like all Classical art-forms, has the necessary object of imparting the combined experience of both *natural* and *artistic*

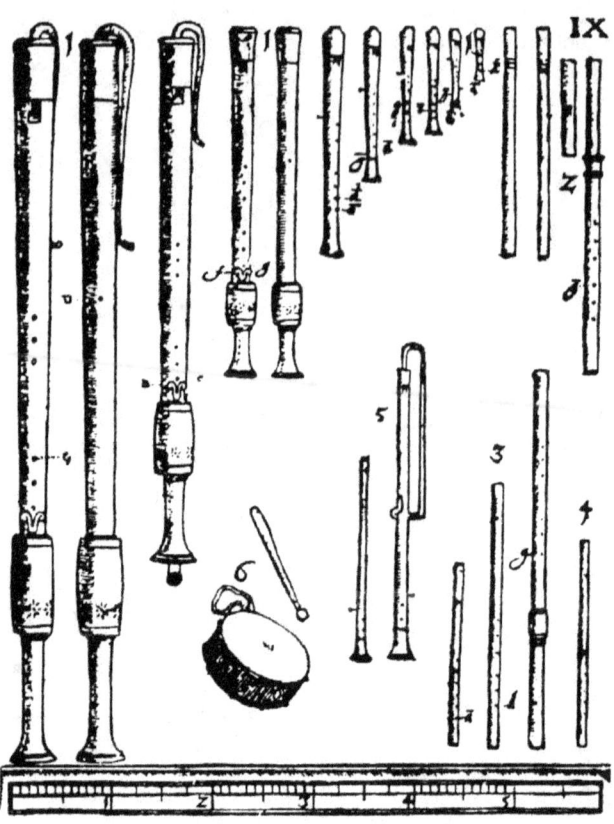

Source: Michael Praetorious, Syntagma Musicum, 1619

FIGURE 4. *By the nature of their construction, the woodwind instruments have registrations which are essentially fixed, even though they can be modified to some degree by choosing alternate fingerings for the same note. The wind instruments therefore tended to be designed and produced in sets or "chests," whose members mostly corresponded to a particular species of singing voice. Above: a woodcut diagram of various wind instruments in use in the early Seventeenth Century.*

beauty.[13] This begs the question: what is the object to which such ideas of beauty correspond? The proper response to the question is Plato's *ideas*,[14] or Gottfried

---

12. Archimedes, "Measurement of a Circle," and "Quadrature of the Parabola," in *The Works of Archimedes,* ed. by T.L. Heath (New York: Dover Publications), pps. 91-98, 233-252.

13. LaRouche, "Classical Idea," *op. cit.*

14. Plato discusses his theory of "ideas" (*eide*) throughout the corpus of his dialogues, and the dialogue *Parmenides* is wholly devoted to its investigation. Primary locations, in assumed general chronology of composition, include: *Meno,* in *Plato: Laches, Protagoras, Meno, Euthydemus,* trans. by W.R.M. Lamb, 81b-87c; *Phaedo,* in *Plato: Euthyphro, Apology, Crito, Phaedo, Phaedrus,* trans. by H.N. Fowler, 72e-80d; *The Republic,* in *Plato: The Republic,* trans by Paul Shorey, Vol. II, 505a-520a; *Parmenides,* in *Plato: Cratylus, Parmenides, Greater Hippias, Lesser Hippias,* trans. by H.N. Fowler, passim.; *Theatetus,* 184b-186e, and *The Sophist,* 248a-258c, both in *Plato: Theatetus and The Sophist,* trans. by H.N. Fowler. All editions are Loeb Classical Library (Cambridge: Harvard University Press); page numbers listed are used universally, however, and will appear as marginal notations in most editions.

Leibniz's *monads,*[15] or Bernhard Riemann's *Geistesmassen,*[16] or my own choice of term, *thought-objects.*[17] The proper subjects of Classical polyphonic compositions, are *musical thought-objects.*

The essential, deeper psychological features of this *Motivführung* revolution cannot become intelligible, without the following *Type* of direct reference to the subject of the *monad,* or *thought-object.* Since music is a form of language implicit in polyphonic forms of poetic vocalization (according to physiologically natural *bel canto* principles), it, as a medium of communication, must choose a subject for its utterance. It is the essential nature of well-tempered polyphonic development, that the subject of a Classical polyphonic composition *cannot be a symbolic treatment of a sensuous object.* It can be only a different type of object, an object of the intelligence, not the senses; it must be a *thought-object.*

It is therefore necessary to detour briefly from music as such, to set forth summarily some crucial points from the referenced "Metaphor" paper.[18]

II.
What Is a 'Thought-Object'?

Humans are the only mortal species of living creatures which is capable of willfully improving, indefinitely, its *potential population-density* (*per capita,* and per square kilometer of average land-area). Those failed cultures so much admired by the anthropologists, are forms of society which, at a certain point, failed to promote ways of life consistent with adequate negentropic rates of scientific and technological progress. Despite the fact that so many cultures have failed in this way, other cultures, which did not fail so, have risen to take the leading place—at least, up to the present time. Thus, despite the fact that so many cultures, in their turn, have failed, the human species as a whole has achieved within its ranks as a whole a net scientific and technological progress, without which civilization would not have survived in any part of this planet.

That faculty, by means of which mankind generates, transmits, and assimilates scientific and technological progress, is the individual person's *divine spark* of potential for rigorous forms of creative reason. This *spark* is the sole basis for the individual person's species-likeness to the Creator; this *spark* is the locus of that quality called *imago viva Dei.* This creative agency, this *spark,* is the origin of *thought-objects.* That creative facility is initially defined, for classroom purposes, in the following way.

As a matter of first approximation, any given level of development of a faction of scientific practice may be described in terms of a consistent, open-ended series of theorems, a set of theorems each and all derivable, formally, from a single, common, integral set of interdependent axioms and postulates. All "crucial," or "fundamental" scientific progress is expressed in formal terms as a radical change in the integral set of such axioms and postulates, underlying the relevant set of mutually consistent theorems.

For example, given an anomalous experimental result (or, analogous observation), attempt to construct a theorem which describes this result from the standpoint of any choice among existing, generally accepted, consistent bodies of *formal* scientific knowledge. For example, repeat the famous, crucial solenoid experiment of Ampère; attempt to define a theorem for all of the significant features of this experimental result, constructing a theorem which is formally consistent with the doctrine of James Clerk Maxwell; it cannot be done![19] It could be done only if a radical change is im-

15. Gottfried Wilhelm Leibniz, **Monadology,** trans. by George Montgomery (LaSalle: Open Court Publishing Co., 1989).

16. See Bernhard Riemann, "Zur Psychologie und Metaphysik," on Herbart's Göttingen lectures, for Riemann's reference to *Geistesmassen,* in **Mathematische Werke,** 2nd. ed. (1892), posthumous papers, ed. by H. Weber in collaboration with R. Dedekind.

17. See Bernhard Riemann, "Zur Psychologie und Metaphysik," on Herbart's Göttingen lectures, for Riemann's reference to *Geistesmassen,* in **Mathematische Werke,** 2nd. ed. (1892), posthumous papers, ed. by H. Weber in collaboration with R. Dedekind.

18. *Ibid.*

19. The topological aspect of the electromagnetic phenomenon is already evident in the simple solenoid experiment of Ampère's early researches: A.M. Ampère, *Theorie mathematique des phenomenes electro-dynamiques uniquement déduite de l'experience* (Paris: Blanchard, 1958).

In the simple apparatus illustrated, the magnetic compass needle will be seen to rotate 360° in a 180° turn of the compass around the electrified solenoid, suggesting a multiply connected topology of action.

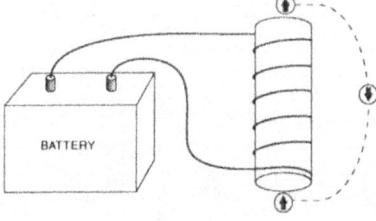

Bernhard Riemann's investigations of toroidal and higher-genus topologies in connection with electrical "streamings" are reported in Felix Klein, **On Riemann's Theory of Algebraic Functions and Their Integrals,** trans. by Frances Hardcastle (Cambridge: MacMillan and Bowes, 1893).

James Clerk Maxwell insisted that such topological features could

posed upon the axiomatic assumptions commonly underlying the dogmas of Clausius, Kelvin, Helmholtz, Grassmann, and Maxwell.[20] In such as the latter case, in which a fair theorem representation for a crucial experiment requires a radical revision of axiomatics, we have an example of the form of a threatened revolution in scientific knowledge.

Consider a simplified, symbolic classroom representation of this point.[21]

---

be ignored for purposes of analysis, and that the higher-genus ("periphractic") regions of space could be reduced to simple connectedness by cuts ("diaphragms"): J.C. Maxwell, *A Treatise on Electricity and Magnetism* (New York: Dover, 1954), §18-22, 481.

A devastating refutation of the entire theory of elasticity upon which the Maxwell electromagnetic theory was based, was given by Eugenio Beltrami in "Sull' equazioni generali dell' elasticitÿ" ("On the General Equations of Elasticity"), *Annali di Matematica pura ed applicata,* serie II, tomo X (1880-82), pp. 188-211; trans. by Richard Sanders, *21st Century Science & Technology,* unpublished.

20. The mathematician Hermann Grassmann constructed the putative mathematical proof for the Rupert Clausius/Lord Kelvin concoction known as the "Second Law of Thermodynamics," and was also employed by Clausius to concoct an incompetent criticism of Bernhard Riemann's work on electrodynamics.

In an 1858 paper, *A Contribution to Electrodynamics,* Riemann asserted the coherence of the theory of electricity and magnetism with that of light and radiant heat, proposing that the electrodynamic effects are not instantaneous, but are propagated with constant velocity equal to the velocity of light. The paper was published posthumously and then criticized by Clausius, who objected to the appearance of an integral expressing the value of the potential, which he interpreted as capable of taking on an infinitesimally small value.

A related criticism was made by Helmholtz against the work of Riemann's collaborator, Wilhelm Weber, the recognized leader in fundamental electrodynamic research. Helmholtz made the irresponsible charge that Weber's Law of Electrical Force contradicted the Law of Conservation of Force, by allowing two attracting charged particles to theoretically achieve an infinite vis viva (energy).

Weber answered the criticism in his *Sixth Memoir on Electrodynamic Measurements,* trans. in *The London, Edinburgh, and Dublin Philosophical Magazine and Journal of Science,* Vol. XLIII—Fourth Series, January-June 1872, pps. 1-20, 119-145. He pointed out that the objection was valid only if the charged particles were allowed an infinite velocity. Thus, Weber deduced that there must be a finite limiting velocity for two electrical particles, such that its square may not exceed c^2. Although Maxwell later renounced Helmholtz's attack in an edition of the *Treatise on Electricity and Magnetism,* the criticism is still found to this day.

An English translation of Riemann's essay, accompanied by a sympathetic summary of Clausius' criticism by the German editor Heinrich Weber, is available in two locations: *International Journal of Fusion Energy,* Vol. 3, No. 1, January 1985, pp. 91-93; and also in Carol White, *Energy Potential* (New York: Campaigner Publications, 1977), pp. 295-300.

21. Lyndon H. LaRouche, Jr., "In Defense of Common Sense," in *The Science of Christian Economy and Other Prison Writings* (Washington, D.C.: Schiller Institute, 1991), pp. 8-41.

Instrumental Imitation of the Singing Voice

In this passage from Mozart's Mass in C, K. 427, the solo soprano voice introduces a phrase which serves as a transition back to the concluding full choral section. The solo soprano is accompanied at the unison by the Violin I, while the Violin II plays a pedal-point B♭. Then the chorus enters during the fifth measure of this example; the choral sopranos sing the same line as the solo soprano before, but the Violin I now plays the line at a displaced range, one octave higher. The Violin II now plays with the sopranos at the unison, and the oboes take over the B♭ pedal point, one and two octaves higher than the previous Violin II pedal point.

Given, a formal system of theorem-point scientific knowledge: an open-ended series of mutually consistent theorems, each and all consistent with an underlying set of intradependent axioms and postulates. Call this a "theorem-lattice." Begin with such a theorem-lattice, A. Introduce a crucial, real-life experiment, X_1, for whose result no theorem may be constructed which is consistent with A.

Now, there exists at least one radical revision of A's underlying set of axioms and postulates, which permits the construction of a formally consistent theorem for X_1; there may exist many such revisions which satisfy this bare condition. However, we must satisfy not only the evidence of X_1; we must also satisfy every crucial experiment which corresponds to the subject of any other theorem of A. This restricts the choices of radical revision for A's axiom-set. In the case this condition is met, we have a new theorem-lattice, B.

Thus, in similar fashion, define a series of mutually inconsistent theorem-lattices, $A, B, C, D, E, \ldots$. Since each theorem-lattice is separated from its predecessor by a radical change in the implicitly underlying set of interdependent axioms and postulates, no two lattices are consistent, and no theorem of one lattice is consistent with any theorem of any other lattice. This is a higher expression of what is termed a "mathematical discontinuity"; in this case, a formally unbridgeable chasm separating each term of the series from every other term of the series.

In the real universe, as reality may be distinguished from mere formalities, the test of the validity of the series, $A, B, C, D, E, \ldots$, is posed by the question, whether the successive changes in modes of society's productive (and, related) behavior, effects resulting from employment of changes in scientific knowledge, do, or do not represent implicitly an increase of the rate of growth of society's potential population-density. In the case that this test is satisfied, the series as a whole represents (and is represented by) *a subsuming method* of generating revolutionary successions of advance in scientific and technological progress.

The advances in productivity (and, potential population-density) which European culture has achieved (over the anti-growth oppositions), during the past 550 years, since the 1439-1440 a.d. Council of Florence, are implicitly the outgrowth of radical axiomatic changes in creative scientific thinking. These changes can be represented most efficiently, most intelligibly from the standpoint of a non-algebraic function's reference-point in a radically constructive synthetic geometry. This history, seen through the eyes of such a non-algebraic geometry, permits the easiest rigorous method for introducing the meaning of *thought-object,* whether for physical science, or for music.

This modern history's most elementary, pivotal discoveries can be reduced to a short list.[22] From ancient Classical Greece (including southern Italy), two geometrical discoveries are outstanding: the famous Pythagorean Theorem, and Plato's extensive treatments of those five regular polyhedra which may be inscribed within a sphere (the "Platonic Solids").[23] The method associated with these discoveries, is the Socratic dialectic, as typified by Plato's **Parmenides** dialogue, a method which Plato stressed as congruent with a radically constructive synthetic geometry.[24] The rise of modern science, resting upon the Greek heritage of Pythagoras, Plato, and Archimedes, begins with the discoveries of Cardinal Nicolaus of Cusa and his collaborators, about 550 years ago, centered around Cusa's **De Docta Ignorantia** (On Learned Ignorance).[25]

The most crucial discoveries in modern physical science occurred during an interval of approximately 250 years, from c. 1440 a.d. through the beginning of the Eighteenth Century. The 1696-1697 a.d. solution to the brachistochrone problem, by Leibniz and the Bernoullis, is typical of the flood of final touches on the first quarter millennium of modern scientific progress.[26] From this period, the following are the most notable. (1) Cusa's 1430's discovery of the "isoperimetric" ("Maximum-Minimum") principle, the root of the later principle of non-algebraic "least action."[27] (2) The further elaboration, by Leonardo da Vinci and his collaborators, of the implications of the "Platonic Solids."[28] (3) The establishing of the first comprehen-

22. LaRouche, "Metaphor," *op. cit.,* pp. 20-22.

23. Plato, **Timaeus,** trans. by R.G. Bury, Loeb Classical Library (Cambridge: Harvard University Press, 1975), 54d-55d, pp. 131-135.

24. For Plato on geometry as dialectic, see Plato, **The Republic,** *op. cit.,* Book 7, 509d-543b.

25. See Nora Hamerman, "The Council of Florence: The Religious Event That Shaped the Era of Discovery," **Fidelio,** Vol. I, No. 2, Spring 1992, pp. 23-26.

26. Gottfried Wilhelm Leibniz, "Specimen Dynamicum" (1695), in **Leibniz Selections,** ed. by Philip P. Wiener (New York: C.S. Sons, 1951); Johann Bernoulli, "Curvatura radii in diaphanis non uniformibus," **Acta Eruditorum,** May 1697, trans. in D.J. Struik, ed., *A Source Book in Mathematics, 1200-1800* (Princeton, N.J.: Princeton University Press, 1968), pp. 391-399.

27. Nicolaus of Cusa, *De Docta Ignorantia, op. cit.,* pp. 53-66.

28. Luca Pacioli, **De Divina Proportione** (1497) (Vienna: 1896), for

sive program in mathematical physics, by Johannes Kepler, principally upon the basis provided by Cusa and Leonardo.[29] (4) The seventeenth-century development of a Keplerian, non-algebraic calculus of physical "least action," by Pierre Fermat,[30] Blaise Pascal,[31] Christiaan Huygens,[32] Gottfried Leibniz, and the Bernoullis.[33] It was in this Renaissance setting of vigorous scientific progress, that the rise of Classical polyphony through Leonardo da Vinci,[34] Bach, Haydn, Mozart, Beethoven, Brahms, *et al.* occurred.

At first inspection, geometric discoveries are apparently, merely mathematical formalities, in the sense algebra is in fact merely empty formalism. We have already indicated here, that the validity of a succession of formal revolutionary discoveries is tested by the yardstick of potential population-density. For obvious reasons, physics, chemistry, and biology, combined as one, insofar as they reflect man's increase in power over nature—*per capita,* and per square kilometer—are an implied approximation of increase of potential population-density. Since the middle of the Fifteenth Century, the development in empirical authority of non-algebraic mathematical science has been premised upon the universal principle of physical least action: least action in physical space-time, a concept rooted in Cusa's isoperimetric, "non-algebraic" circle, the least (circular) perimetric displacement subsuming the relatively largest area. Throughout that 250 years or so, this principle of (physical) least action has been situated in respect to two interdependent physical phenomena: electromagnetic radiation and hydrodynamics. Even today, all sound experimental physics relies upon those non-algebraic species of formal functions which locate physical reality in terms of the hydrodynamics of electromagnetic least action.

It is in that setting, of geometrical and physical thought, combined, that the easiest definition of a

which Leonardo da Vinci drew the geometrical diagrams. Reproductions of these drawings appear in *The Unknown Leonardo,* ed. by Ladislao Reti (New York: McGraw-Hill Book Company, 1974), pp. 70-71.

29. See, for example, Johannes Kepler, *Mysterium Cosmographicum* (*The Secret of the Universe*), trans. by A.M. Duncan (New York: Abaris Books, 1981), p. 93: "For in one respect Nicholas of Cusa and others seem to me divine, that they attached so much importance to the relationship between a straight line and a curved line and dared to liken a curve to God, a straight line to his creatures...."

30. Pierre Fermat, *Oeuvres Fermat,* ed. 1891, epistl. xlii, xliii.

31. Blaise Pascal, *L'oeuvre de Pascal,* ed. by Jacques Chevalier (Paris: Gallimard, 1954).

32. Christiaan Huygens, *The Pendulum Clock, or Geometrical Demonstrations Concerning the Motion of Pendula as Applied to Clocks,* trans. by Richard J. Blackwell (Ames: Iowa State University Press, 1986), passim; also, *Treatise on Light* (1690), trans. by Sylvanus P. Thompson (New York: Dover Publications, 1962).

33. See footnote 26.

34. In his lifetime, Leonardo was as famous as a musician as he was as an artist and engineer. Although the book *De Voce* (On the Voice) which Leonardo is presumed to have written is lost, the available codices provide crucial examples of his thinking, practice, and great influence upon the subsequent development of composition and design of stringed instruments.

   The most comprehensive reference is Emanuel Winternitz, *Leonardo da Vinci as a Musician* (New Haven: Yale University Press, 1982). Not only was Leonardo closely associated with the leading instrument makers of his day, but he was a celebrated virtuoso performer on the *lira da braccio,* a stringed, bowed instrument which is universally regarded as one of the closest forerunners of the violin. In its fully developed form it had a flat body, rounded shoulders, and five melody strings which could be stopped against the fingerboard, as well as two open strings that ran freely through the air outside the fingerboard and would sound only their full length when touched by the bow or plucked by the player's fingers. It was held against the upper arm, had a softer sound than the modern violin, and was used for polyphonic accompaniment (usually improvised) to the singing of poetry.

   Leonardo's interest in the design of instruments that could imitate and amplify vocal choral polyphony, is further exemplified by his work on inventing a "viola organista," a keyboard instrument analogous to the organ. Instead of producing the tones by wind, the "viola organista" used an arrangement by which the keys would activate a continuous bow across the strings, thus imitating an ensemble of viols.

   One of the earliest recorded musical inventions of Leonardo is a "lira" (presumably, a *lira da braccio*) in the unusual shape of a horse's skull, which he presented to the ruler of Milan, Ludovico Sforza, in 1482. This attempt to create a more resonant stringed instrument by utilizing the cavities of the skull, albeit in this case an animal skull, is

highly suggestive with regard to Leonardo's perception of the relationship between sound production in the voice and in stringed instruments—especially since Leonardo was the first to identify, in his drawings of the human skull from around 1490, the sinus cavities which play a key role in defining registers and amplifying the voice.

   The violin itself emerged at some point in the first half of the sixteenth century. In addition to omitting the two free strings, relative to the *lira da braccio* it reduced the number of melody strings to four and introduced the famous arched shape of the case, which gave the violin a capability of reproducing the intensity of the *bel canto* singing voice. In an essay reprinted in his 1967 book *Musical Instruments and their Symbolism in Western Art* (New Haven, Yale University Press, 1967), Winternitz presented the hypothesis that the first actual violin may be the invention of the painter Gaudenzio Ferrari, who depicts a clearly identifiable violin being played by an angel in a frescoed vault in Saronno, a town not far from Milan. While Gaudenzio was not a direct pupil of Leonardo, he was part of the Lombard school that had been shaped by Leonardo's influence during his two long sojourns in Milan, and he shared Leonardo's range of interests in painting, singing, and musical instrument development. Cremona, the city where the violin family of stringed instruments was perfected from the later sixteenth through the eighteenth centuries, is within this same Leonardo-influenced Lombard region. The imprint of Leonardo's influence on the visual arts is stamped throughout the region, and there is no reason to believe it would be any different for musical instruments.

thought-object may be supplied. From that vantage-point, in turn, the nature of a musical thought-object follows readily. Resume the elaboration of the theorem-lattice series.

Given, the indicated series of theorem-lattices, *A, B, C, D, E,* . . . . Define a function which subsumes the generation of the successive terms of this series. Since no two terms of the series may be consistent, no formal function for the series can be defined by means of the terms denoting specific theorem-lattices. Rather, even by mere definition, the generation of *B* from *A, C* from *B,* and so on, lies in that which generates the *absolute* quality of formal discontinuity between any two terms of this series. That generation is the *radical change* in axiomatics, so altering the implicitly underlying set of interdependent axioms and postulates.

There is a "mapping correspondence" between this agency of radical change and the discontinuities separating the terms of the series. Those radical changes correspond to thought-objects. That is what we must define, before returning to the musical thought-objects.

There are two distinct species of thought-objects implied in the given, illustrative series of theorem-lattices. First, on the relatively lower level, there is a quality of the thought-object which is typified by the transformation of *A* to generate *B.* Second, there is the higher quality, higher species of thought-object associated with a notion of a choice of determined ordering for the series presented, the ordering of the lower-order thought-objects corresponding to the discontinuities $\overline{AB}, \overline{BC}, \overline{CD}, \overline{DE},$. . . .

For example, a successfully advancing science would be associated with a succession of such revolutions, each always leading the relevant society (implicitly) to higher levels of potential population-density. This would also signify, that that generation of successive revolutions $\overline{AB}$ and $\overline{BC}$ must result in a revolution $\overline{CD}$ which latter increases the *potential* population-density more rapidly than the average of $\overline{AB}$ and $\overline{BC}$. These successive revolutions are effected under the guidance of a self-evolving method for effecting successive such revolutions, a self-evolving method of scientific discovery. Call this quality of revolutionary ordering a method of *evolutionary negentropy* in increase of potential population-density.

Understand "evolutionary negentropy" as a conception introduced by Nicolaus of Cusa.[35] The progressive evolution of the biosphere is dominated by emergence of relatively higher species—higher than any previously extant. This does not (generally) wipe out the surpassed inferior species. Rather, the proliferation of most among the accumulated, interacting species makes possible the emergent existence of the higher species. Similarly, in the case of the Mendeleyev Periodic Table of Elements and their Isotopes, the emergence of helium and lithium, and so on, from nuclear fusion of hydrogen, and so on, does not eliminate the lower ranking elements and isotopes of that table; rather, that development is characteristic of an ever higher state of organization of the "table" as an interdependent wholeness.

We combine this view of such revolutionary/evolutionary processes as these, with a notion of rising "free energy" of the entire "system" undergoing such ordered evolution. This combination of higher states of organization with relative increase of "free energy," is a definition we prescribe for our use of the term "negentropy."

Thus, we have our two species of thought-objects, relative to our illustrative series of formal theorem-lattices. The first, relatively lower species, is associated with the *Type*[36] of discontinuities separating *A* from *B,* and so on. The second species, a cousin of the *Motivführung* principle, is associated with the *relative evolutionary negentropy* of the whole series as a *determined* series as a whole.

There exists no medium of communication within whose terms either species of thought-object might be represented *explicitly.* No form of algebra, nor of other species of formal language-medium, could represent such a thought-object *explicitly.* Thought-objects belong to a class of distinct mental existences which have no functional correspondence, or equivalence to those representable sensory images which are the type of explicit objects of formal communication.

---

35. In "The Vision of God" (1464), Nicolaus of Cusa develops the con-

ception that each species, with its natural faculties as they develop, "yearns" for the existence of a higher species, as man does for the knowledge of the Absolute, of God. Here, Cusa's idea of negentropic species-evolution as the characteristic of Creation, is expressed by the poetic conception of *terminus specie.* The universe consists of negentropic growth of higher orderings, whose microcosm is human reason. The species recognizes this divine order of Creation, in its own way, and becomes a singularity in the transition from one ordering to the next. Thus, the species has a *terminus specie,* the actualization of infinity in one point, which enables further development.

36. LaRouche, "Metaphor," *op. cit.*, pp. 26-32.

The same is true, of course, of musical thought-objects, such as the thought-objects corresponding to any among the three principal discoveries upon which the *Motivführung* revolution depends. This is to emphasize, that that creative faculty, the means by which Leonardo da Vinci effected his fundamental scientific discoveries was the same higher, ("negentropic") *methodological* thought-object which directed his principal compositions in music[37] and plastic arts. Notably, in the plastic arts, Leonardo's medium of discovery was that same set of geometrical principles governing his fundamental discoveries in physical science.

Yet, in both aspects of Leonardo's creative output, no mere symbolic device could represent the relevant thought-object. Nonetheless, there do exist indirect means for communication of thought-objects, with certainty, from one mind to another. Ironically—"ironical" in a most meaningful dual sense—these indirect means, known as Plato's "Socratic," or "dialectical" method, are more efficient agencies for communication than any formal medium could become. Not only is the Socratic dialectic more efficient than the banal, nominalist Aristotelian formalism; the Socratic dialectic efficiently imparts those classes of conceptions which are so powerful, so profound, that the gnostic Aristotelians, such as Immanuel Kant, avow these conceptions to be intrinsically "unknowable."[38] These thought-objects are otherwise known as "Platonic ideas."[39]

Classical music demands a method of polyphonic composition equivalent to that Socratic dialectic. This method, applied to that developed form of the musical medium, is employed to the effect of imparting, indirectly, a sub-class of otherwise "unutterable Platonic ideas," called usefully either "musical ideas," or, with less ambiguity, "musical thought-objects."

The point has been reached, here, to identify the class of phenomena of inner mental experience which contain the marks of the thought-object.

---

37. See note 34.

38. Immanuel Kant, *Critique of Judgment*, trans. by J.H. Bernard (New York: Hafner Press, 1951), p. 152ff. See Friedrich Schiller's refutation of Kant in his "Letters on the Aesthetic Education of Man," in *Friedrich Schiller, Poet of Freedom,* ed. by William F. Wertz, Jr., Vol. I (Washington, D.C.: Schiller Institute, 1985), pp. 251-255; and in "On Grace and Dignity," Vol. II (1988), pp. 365-368; "Aesthetical Lectures (1792-1793)," Vol . II (1988), pp. 471-481; "Kallias or, On the Beautiful," Vol. II (1988), pp. 482-526.

39. Formally, Plato's *eidos* is correctly translated as the English "idea"; in other words, Plato means what Leibniz identifies by *monads,* and I by "thought-objects."

III.
The Principle of Least Action

Let us resume here with a partial restatement of what has been said thus far. The crucial feature of the Christian "Golden Renaissance's" launching of modern science, approximately 550 years ago, is Nicolaus of Cusa's discovery of his isoperimetric ("Maximum-Minimum") principle.[40] As this Renaissance picked up from the point at which Classical Greek civilization had been interrupted, that by the evil, Gaia-Python-Dionysos-Apollo Cult of Delphi,[41] so, Cusa began the modern scientific revolution at approximately the point Archimedes' work was snuffed out by the brutish legionnaires of Delphi's pagan Rome[42]: Archimedes' paradoxical theorems on the subject of "squaring the circle."[43] This crucial discovery by Cusa is aptly described, alternately, as a unique physical principle of "least action"; so, it appears more clearly in retrospect, by the close of the Seventeenth Century. This comparison of two discoveries, presented in 1440 and 1697, respectively, serves us here as our exemplary choice of model for a thought-object.

On closer, stricter scrutiny, the term "squaring the circle" is ambiguous. Its cruder meaning is, simply: to construct a square whose area is nearly equal to that of a given circle. This task was solved, implicitly, by Ar-

---

40. *De Docta Ignorantia, op. cit.,* vol. I.

41. Although the temple of the oracle of Delphi is usually identified with the cult of Apollo, even in Classical Greek times, Apollo was only one of the three pagan deities with which the complex was associated. The original deities of the site were, quite literally, Satan and his mother, known respectively by the local aliases, *Python* and *Gaia.* Python also used locally his Phrygian alias, *Dionysus,* in ancient times, through the time of the famous Delphi priest of Apollo, the biographer Plutarch, the oracle was a priestess who was assigned the name of *Pythia,* signifying her position as a priestess of Python. She delivered her utterances at the grave-site of Python-Dionysus. Later, after the service, the priests of Apollo provided the explanatory "spin" on the oracle's enigmatic messages. Python-Dionysus was equivalent to the Indian sub-continent's *Shiva,* the Semitic *Satan,* and the Hellenistic *Osiris;* this Dionysus was the Satan worshipped by that forerunner of New Ager Adolf Hitler, self-avowed anti-Christ, Friedrich Nietzsche. For Nietzsche's profession of being Dionysus the anti-Christ, see Friedrich Nietzsche, "Why I Am a Fatality" and *passim.* in "Ecce Homo," in *The Philosophy of Nietzsche* (New York: Modern Library, 1954), pp. 923-933.

42. The City of Rome rose to power among the Latins, and then in Italy, through the intervention of its patron the cult of Delphi. Roman legionnaires murdered Archimedes in B.C. 212.

43. See footnote 12. Cusa probably acquired his copy of Archimedes' writings from the Greek collection brought to Florence by George Gemisthos ("Plethon").

chimedes and others.[44] There is, however, a subtler feature. This subtler task is, to construct the perimeter of a circle by linear, or "algebraic" methods; this second, subtler task is an impossible one, for reasons shown conclusively in a solution constructed by Nicolaus of Cusa. That latter solution is the point of reference for our constructive, indirect, but rigorous definition of a thought-object.

These various points are each and all clarified by closer scrutiny of Archimedes' Four Theorems on the squaring of the circle; this is the approach employed successfully by Cusa.[45] We now describe this summarily.[46]

Inscribe a square within a circle. Circumscribe that circle with a second square (see **Figure 5**). Double the number of sides of each square to form a pair of a regular octagons in the same relationship to the circle as the pair of squares. Repeat the doubling action, to reach a large value of 2^n sides. Look at the region of the circle's perimeter associated with three or four sides of an inscribed polygon of very many sides (**Figure 6**). By estimating the area of both the inscribed and circumscribed polygons, respectively, and by averaging the two areas, we have a rough estimate for the area of the circle; however, the perimeter of neither polygon could ever become congruent with the perimeter of the circle.

Let the diameter of a given circle be one meter. Dividing the estimated perimeter of the circle by one meter, gives us an estimated value for π. However, respecting either polygon, even if we increase the number of sides of an 2^n-sided regular polygon to the astronomical $n=256$, there would remain a well-defined, distinct, functionally determined discrepancy in area between the polygon and the circle. Worse, the many-angular perimeter of the polygon becomes ever less congruent in *species-form* with a circular perimeter. The circle belongs to a different, higher species than any polygon—than any figure derived from so-called Euclidean types of axiomatic ontological assumptions respecting *point* and *straight-line pathways of action.*

Cusa's revolutionary insight into the formal evidence, reflects the fact, that he was a student of Plato and Archimedes, that he rejected the gnostic dogma of Aristotle.[47] Crucial to Cusa's insight, is the Platonic principle of "Socratic negation." The fact, that the circle is not only a different species, but also a higher one, is shown *negatively.* There is then a mental leap, it appears, to the resulting conclusion: the discovery of a new definition of the circle, the *isoperimetric* conception, or as Cusa defines it, his "Maximum-Minimum" principle.[48] However, appearances aside, this discovery is no "blind leap of faith"; Cusa was already a master of Plato's Socratic method; he was familiar with "Platonic ideas."

The remainder of the ensuing two-and-one-half

44. For the work of Archimedes, see footnote 12. For a summary of the Egyptian method of squaring the circle, see Carl B. Boyer, *A History of Mathematics,* 2nd ed., revised by Uta C. Merzbach (New York: John Wiley & Sons, 1991), Chapter 2.
45. Nicolaus of Cusa, *De Circuli Quadratura, op. cit.*
46. LaRouche, "Metaphor," *op. cit.*, pp. 18-20.

47. See below, Section IV.
48. See footnote 27.

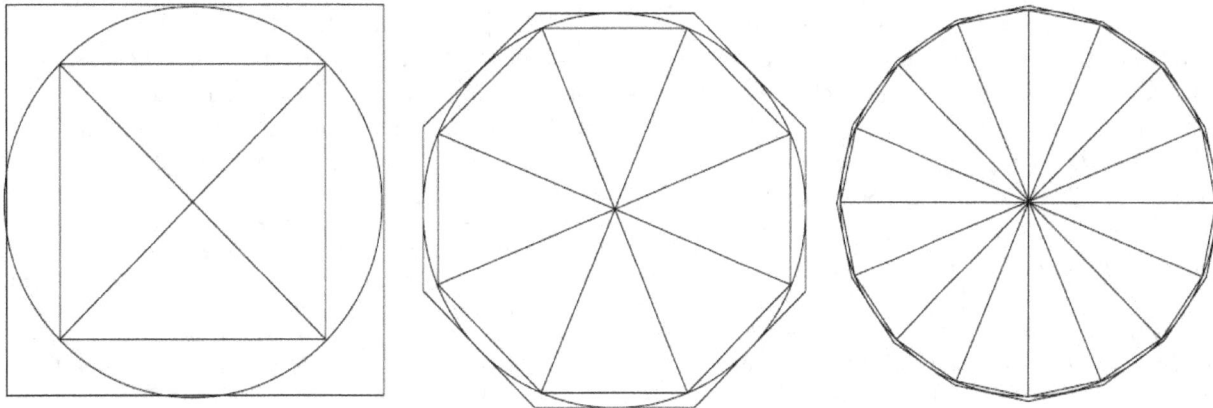

FIGURE 5. *"Squaring the circle": Estimating the area of a square approximately equal to that of a given circle, as the average area of two regular polygons.*

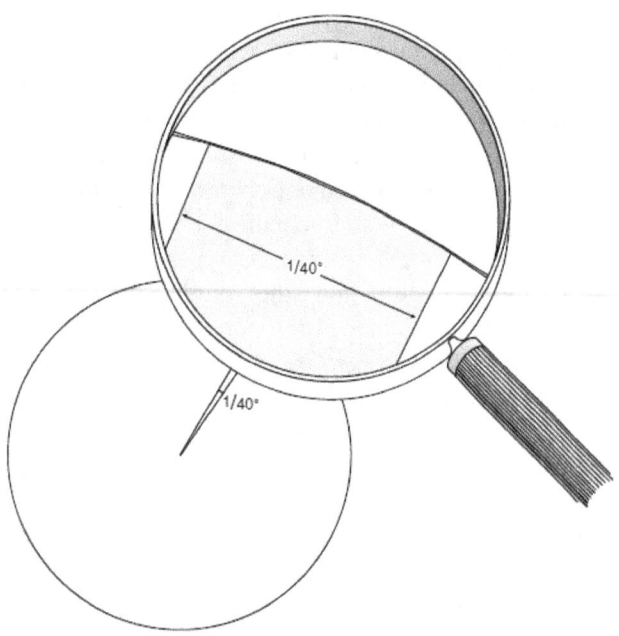

FIGURE 6. *An inscribed polygon of 2^{16} (65,536) sides may seem to closely approach a circle. But the perimeter of the polygon can never become congruent with the circle's perimeter.*

centuries of fundamental scientific progress, was an elaboration of Cusa's isoperimetric principle as the emerging, universal principle of physical least action. Some preliminary observations on this connection are needed, to clear the way for our next major point.

During the Nineteenth Century, the famous Professor Jacob Steiner, the author of the synthetic geometry curriculum for quality secondary schools,[49] contributed a standard classroom demonstration of the iterative, isoperimetric construction of a circle. Although the Steiner construction helps, it must be used as a kind of *negative* demonstration, and not positive determination of the circle as a species. There is no formal way in which the isoperimetric circle might be generated positively from the standpoint of a Euclidean theorem-lattice.[50] The notion of the isoperimetric circle becomes "as if" self-evident, replacing thus axiomatically the no longer self-evident, merely derivative point and straight line. Steiner's construction *does not prove* Cusa's isoperimetric principle; it illustrates the result negatively,

and this from the standpoint of a good quality of secondary-school classroom. After Cusa, the greatest, most fruitful scientific thinkers, beginning with Leonardo da Vinci, treated the circle (and the sphere) as species which exist "self-evidently," and treated other forms as existences which must be derived, by construction, from the point of origin of circular (and spherical) isoperimetric action (in physical space-time). This work focused upon the anomalies of perspective and vision from the vantage-point of origin of isoperimetric, or "least action."

The first next major step for science, was exploring the implications of the "Platonic Solids." This resulted in such crucial accomplishments as the Leonardo-Kepler functional distinction between the two curvatures (positive and negative) of the circle and sphere.[51] The next crucial step, was the elaboration of an isoperimetric, least-action principle for light, by Fermat, Huygens, Leibniz, and the Bernoullis, an elaboration premised, inclusively, upon Leonardo's principles of hydrodynamics.[52] The crucial step forward, in the matter of least-action principles of reflection and refraction, was the seventeenth-century study of the cycloids, this becoming the explicit basis, principally, for the elaboration of non-algebraic functions.

Consider the second example of the generation of a thought-object, before bringing under closer scrutiny the characteristics of thought-objects as such. The cycloids are characterized essentially as the results of *axiomatically circular action upon axiomatically circular action*. These represent the original, primary form of developable function in the physical domain; they serve, thus, as the axiomatic basis for synthetic-geometrical representation of physical processes as phenomena. This circular action is deemed axiomatic, so, replacing in this way the now merely derived existences of point and straight line. The relatively most elementary *ontological* results of such circular action upon circular action, are twofold: first, least-action function as a characteristic of all action in physical space-time (see

49. Jacob Steiner, **Geometrical Constructions with a Ruler, Given a Fixed Circle with Its Center,** trans. by Marion Elizabeth Stark (New York: Scripta Mathematica, Yeshiva University, 1950). Steiner was Bernhard Riemann's instructor in geometry.

50. Euclid, *The 13 Books of the Elements,* trans. by T.L. Heath (New York: Dover Publications, 1956).

51. Lyndon H. LaRouche Jr., **A Concrete Approach to U.S. Science Policy,** (Washington, D.C.: Schiller Institute, 1992).

52. See Carlo Zammattio, "The Mechanics of Water and Stone," in **The Unknown Leonardo,** op. cit., pp. 190-207, for diagrams and citations to the various Leonardo manuscripts and codices; see also Dino De Paoli, "Leonardo: Father of Modern Science," in **Campaigner,** Vol. XV, No. 1, October 1985, pp. 34-37, for a review of Leonardo's investigations into fluid mechanics from a Riemannian standpoint. Leonardo's researches into hydrodynamics were assembled by F.L. Arconati in **Del moto e misura dell'acqua** (1643).

Figure 7); and, second, an affirmation of Kepler's distinction between functions determined, respectively, by negative and positive spherical curvatures (see **Figure 8**).[53] Situate Bernoulli's 1697 treatment of the least-action equivalence of the *brachistochrone* to Huygens' *tautochrone,* in this context (see **Figure 9**).[54]

The result, the proof that radiation of light occurs in a universe which is curved relativistically, in physical space-time premised elementarily upon uniquely axiomatic least action, is a thought-object solution developed, in the late Seventeenth Century, as if by a leap of faith, from a process of Socratic negative reasoning driven rigorously to its limits.

In each of the listed cases of discovery, three general results dominate. Firstly, each, Cusa's, Leonardo's, Kepler's, Huygens', Leibniz's, and the Bernoullis', is generated by the same type of apparent "leap of faith," under analogous circumstances. These circumstances are a paradox driven toward its limit, by means of an exhaustively rigorous application of Socratic dialectical negation, a negation analogous to the method of Plato's **Parmenides**. Secondly, excepting Cusa, who depends upon ancient crucial discoveries, none of the other discoveries listed had been possible without all of

its predecessors in that same series. Thirdly, each discovery, and all combined the more so, increased greatly mankind's power over nature, mankind's potential population-density.

The 1890's work of Georg Cantor,[55] David Hilbert's formalist error on proposing his famous "Tenth Problem,"[56] and the case of Kurt Gödel's famous proof, all illustrate deeper implications of our deceptively simple series of theorem-lattices, *A, B, C, D, E, ...*

Let us substitute for the commas in that series, the letter μ, to such effect that we have, in first approxima-

---

53. Johannes Kepler, *On the Six-Cornered Snowflake,* trans. and ed. by Colin Hardie (Oxford: Clarendon Press, 1966), reprinted by *21st Century Science & Technology,* 1991.

54. See footnote 25.

55. *Georg Cantors Gesammelte Abhandlungen,* ed. by Ernst Zermelow, (Hildesheim, 1962); also, *Beiträge zur Begründung der transfiniten Mengenlehrer,* (Contributions to the Founding of the Theory of Transfinite Numbers), trans. by Philip E.B. Jourdain (New York: Dover Publications, 1955), pp. 282-356.

56. In 1931, the Austrian mathematician Kurt Gödel demonstrated, by formal means, that one can formulate propositions within a formal logical system, the truth of which cannot be determined within the rules of that system. Gödel's proof served as an answer, in the negative, to the "Second Problem" of the famous twenty-three unsolved problems which Göttingen University mathematician David Hilbert had proposed in 1900 to the Second International Mathematical Congress in Paris. Hilbert's "Second Problem" was to determine whether it can be proved that the axioms of arithmetic are consistent—that is, can never lead to contradictory results. The same formal premise lay behind many of Hilbert's questions, including the "Tenth Problem," which concerns the solvability of Diophantine equations (algebraic equations in which the coefficients and solutions must be integers). For Hilbert's "Tenth Problem," see Carl B. Boyer, *A History of Mathematics, op. cit.,* pp. 610-614. See also Ernest Nagel and James R. Newman, *Gödel's Proof* (New York: New York University Press, 1958).

FIGURE 7. *The least-action principle embedded in cycloid functions.*

In his 1673 On the Pendulum Clock, *Huygens demonstrated that a pendulum made to follow the path of a cycloid (curve MPI) will have the same period, no matter what the amplitude of the swing— that is, the cycloid is "tautochronic."*

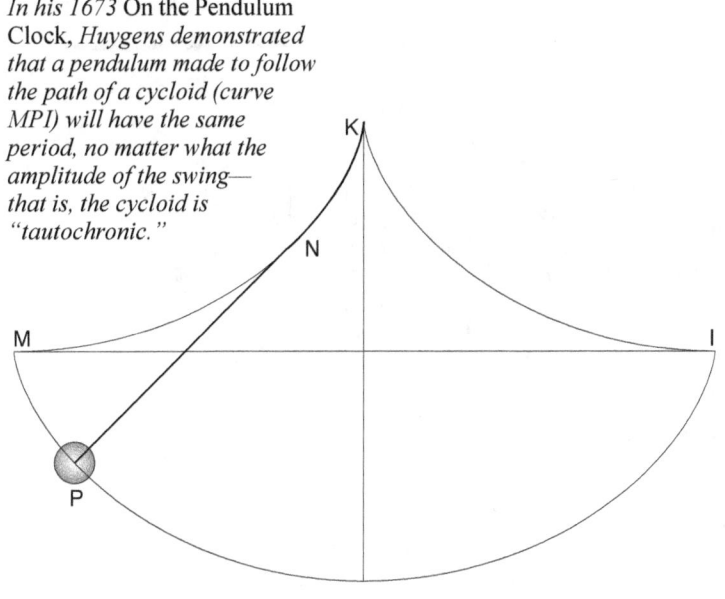

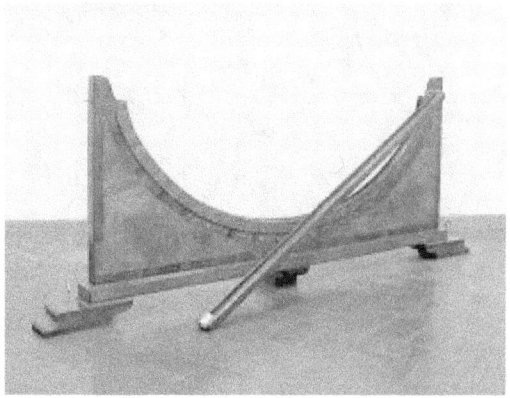

A ball rolling down a cycloidal track will reach the bottom in the same time, no matter where on the track it is released. Later, Johann Bernoulli demonstrated that the cycloid also has the property of a "brachistochrone"—it is the least-time pathway. (Model in the Museum of the History of Science, Florence, Italy.)

tion, the new representation of that series, μ_{ab}, μ_{bc}, μ_{cd}, ... Each of the terms now appears to correspond to a successful "leap of faith," to Kant's purportedly "unknowable" agency of creative discovery. This cannot yet be an adequate representation; two general grounds of that warning are to be indicated. Firstly, without the discoverer's earlier reproduction of numerous similar "leaps of faith" of his predecessors, his own "leap of faith" were impossible, rather than successful, as it was. Secondly, this functional (e.g., *analysis situs*) ordering of the formal series correlates with a twofold increase of mankind's potential *per-capita* power over nature: on account of the individual discovery, as such, and, also, additionally, on account of the contribution to the increased power for discovery by society in general.

Shift our view, momentarily, to the Classical humanist classrooms of Europe, from the Grootean teaching order, the Brothers of the Common Life, through the German *Gymnasium* of Wilhelm von Humboldt's design. The relevant feature of that classroom, is emphasis upon use of primary sources' representation of processes of great discovery, prompting the student, in this way, to replicate that mental experience of the discoverer in the student's own mental processes.

The act of discovery is not represented explicitly in any primary source. That action is not explicitly representable in any medium of communication. Nonetheless, a fair replica of the original act of discovery may be evoked from within the creative potential of the student's mental processes. In that degree, that aspect of the creative intellects of Pythagoras, Plato, Archimedes, Cusa, Kepler, and so on, lives anew as an integral capability of the mind of the student. So, it may be said fairly, the noble dead may communicate, by such dialectical indirection, as if directly, mind to mind, with

(a)

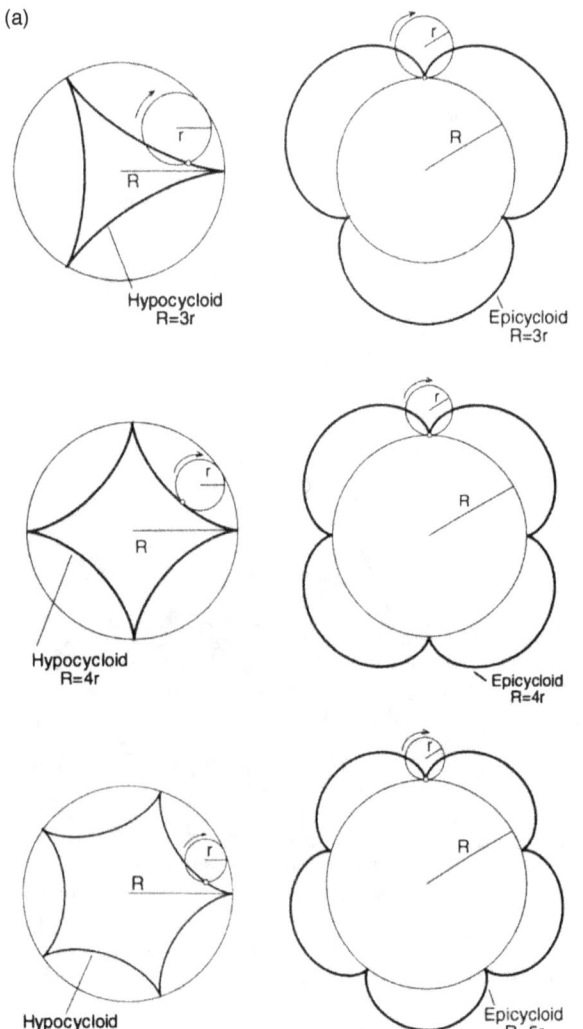

(b)

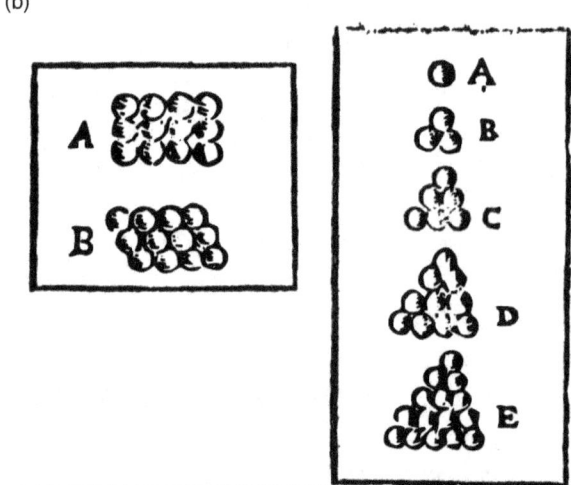

FIGURE 8. *Positive and negative curvature. (a) The figures derived by rolling a circle on the interior of a larger circle (hypocycloids) are of a different species than those produced by rolling it on the exterior of the same circle (epicycloids). (b) Packing of spheres, as illustrated in Kepler's "On the Six-Cornered Snowflake."*

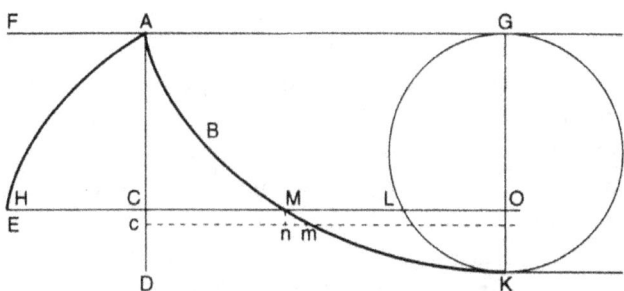

FIGURE 9. *In 1697, Johann Bernoulli demonstrated that cycloid AMK had both the "tautochronic" property shown by Huygens, and the property of a "brachistochrone"—that is, it is the least-action, least-time pathway of descent.*

the living. Such is true education, unlike that sterile textbook drill and grill, which rehearses today's pupils to pass computer-scoreable multiple-choice questionnaires. Thus, by the methods of Christian humanist education, the quality of true "genius" is learned, by incorporating in one's own creative-mental processes a choice selection of bits of the mental processes of a large number of the greatest discoverers, such as Plato, of mankind's past.

Consider the exemplary case of one of the greatest thinkers in all recorded history, Nicolaus of Cusa. His education was shaped by the influence of that great Grootean teaching order, the Brothers of the Common Life. He assimilated thus, for example, the minds of Plato and Archimedes, and many others. Or the illustrious case of Leibniz's collaborator, Christiaan Huygens.[57] Christiaan's father, Constantine, was a celebrated Dutch diplomat, a co-sponsor of the young Rembrandt van Rijn, and one-time ambassador to London. In London, father and son Huygens gained access to the royal collection of Leonardo da Vinci's papers, whose contents played later a direct part in important work of both Christiaan Huygens and Leibniz.[58] The work of Cusa was known to these circles; the work of Kepler dominated the Seventeenth Century, and was later, the foundation for much of the work of Carl Friedrich Gauss. Leibniz's founding of the first successful differ-

ential calculus, circa 1676, in Paris, France,[59] was, like other attempts of that period, prompted explicitly by Kepler, and contained the work toward that end in Leibniz's study of Blaise Pascal's unpublished notes, as well as Pascal's published work. Consider, to similar effect, two Platonic dialogues composed by Leibniz for the stated purpose of demonstrating that crucial issues of science today require resort to Plato's dialectical method.

Science is not the sterile pedagogue's obsession with statistical procedures for "inductive" generalization from a caddis-fly pupa's aggregation of so-called "facts" and recipes. Science is, historically, the development and interaction of those higher species of mental life which are here designated as the thought-objects, generated by creative activity, which Leibniz termed *monads*.

All of us who have effected successfully some discovery of a natural principle, as this reviewer did, decades ago in his contributions to the science of physical economy,[60] know that thought-objects are fully intelligible, although not susceptible of an explicit, sensory form of representation in any formal medium of communication. We also know that our successful work is modeled, as if "heuristically," upon our learning experience in reproducing within our own creative mental processes the thought-objects corresponding to valid acts of discovery of principle by as many as possible among all the greatest thinkers before our time.

Thus, the provisional array of such thought-objects, μ_{ab}, μ_{bc}, μ_{cd}, ..., is subsumed by a generative, self-evolving quality of yet higher-order thought-object. This higher species of such thought-object is called *scientific method,* a thought-object whose efficient dimensionalities are the notion of "evolutionary negentropy," which we referenced above.

IV.
Musical Thought-Objects

In its most essential features, what we may say of thought-objects, as in scientific work, we may say also of musical thought-objects. The J.S. Bach *Musical Offering* underscores the place of a major/minor-key cross-over *dissonance*—e.g., a formal discontinuity—

---

57. In 1672, Gottfried Leibniz was appointed to what we would term today a "fellowship" to minister Jean-Baptiste Colbert's Paris-based French Royal Academy of Science, where he began his long association with Christiaan Huygens.

58. For example, Huygens made use of Leonardo's construction of the aberration in a spherical mirror in the closing pages of his ***Treatise on Light*** (New York: Dover Publications, 1962), p. 127.

59. Gottfried Wilhelm Leibniz, "History and Origin of the Differential Calculus," in ***The Early Mathematical Manuscripts of Leibniz,*** trans. by J.M. Child (LaSalle: Open Court Publishing Co., 1920).

60. The essential features of the author's 1948-1952 discoveries are restated within "On the Subject of Metaphor," *op. cit.*

in the process of composition. The subsumption of many resolved discontinuities under the governance of a single, well-defined ordering-principle for that succession as a whole, presents us, in the instance of any single such composition, with a process analogous to the idealized theorem-lattice, *A, B, C, D, E, ...*

As long as the composer adheres strictly to the natural lawfulness of *Classical* well-tempered, *bel canto*-rooted instrumental, and vocal polyphony as polyphony, certain dissonances, such as the F♯ of those Classical C-major/C-minor *Motivführung* compositions quoting from Bach's *Musical Offering,* are defined meaningfully as formal discontinuities, to be resolved as such. (In strict Romanticism, or atonalism, such rationality is more or less irrelevant.) Thus, the composer's *Motivführung* solution to the *negation* so represented thematically (as in quotations from the *Musical Offering,* by Mozart, Beethoven, Schubert, Chopin, *et al.*), generates a species of *musically-defined* thought-object, or, briefly, a musical thought-object.

The definitional significance of such a musical thought-object as musical, rather than simply a thought-object, is the following. Firstly, even the individual thought-objects, *of a series,* within a succession, are provoked, in the individual's sovereign creative mental processes, by the polyphonic lawfulness of the Classical, well-tempered musical medium. Secondly, the ordering of a series of such thought-objects, as a composition, or part of it, is a higher-order thought-object, which latter is defined, generated by a negative feature of a process of composition. The natural rules of polyphony flowing from singing voices of the most natural training (i.e., *bel canto*) are the basis for defining an anomaly, and, thus, are the basis for the generation of a musical thought-object. In other words, the thought-object is referenced in respect to its place in the development occurring in the musical medium. Since only the Classical mode of composition permits this determination, those musical thought-objects are defined in respect to the Classical form of the medium.

"Show me your thought-object, by indicating to me how this [musical] passage should be performed," would be the way a trained Classical performer would tend to reference the matter being addressed in the foregoing paragraphs. Commonly, among such professionals, it is the shadow of the thought-object, so to speak, which is referenced, not the thought-object as such. The formal heading under which this reference is made, would be, most frequently, "musical insight," a quality whose exact communication may be suggested by apt description, but whose conception is recognized by performance of a relevant musical passage or composition. We may refer to the passage, or the composition as a whole, and speak of a performance-demonstrated insight into the *intent* of that passage; we speak of this as musical "insight."

The pleasure of such musical ideas—musical thought-objects—is akin to that of solving a scientific problem: it is the quality of emotion we associate with "sacred love" (*agapē, caritas*), as distinct from sensuous, object-fixed "profane love." In that respect, all Classical polyphony, all Classical musical ideas (thought-objects), as opposed to the erotic fantasies of Wagner's and Mahler's "Romanticism," have an intrinsic quality akin to the religious feeling of the **Gospel** of St. John and St. Paul's **I Corinthians** 13.

In each instance of the series of fundamental scientific discoveries referenced, the most rigorous principles of geometric construction, driving a paradox to its limit, was required—as in Plato's *Parmenides*—to show the ontologically *axiomatic* issue upon whose resolution the matter hangs. In this setting, and only such, is a valid thought-object generated by the individual mind's sovereignly creative agency. In music, similarly, a strictly lawful polyphony, itself rooted in strictly well-tempered, (Florentine)[61] *bel canto* vocalization, is the "constructive geometry of hearing," by means of which the relevant axiomatic issues are posed to the creative agency.

This requirement's character is illustrated by the following exemplary problems of musical performance. There are several, broadly mandatory features of a competent Classical performance, for lack of which rigor the necessary, *indirect* communication of the composer's intended musical thought-object will be impaired, or even may not occur (it should be noted that this does not apply to the performance of Romantic, or atonal compositions, whose subjects are not thought-objects, but rather the smarmy, erotic objects of the

---

61. It is a fact cut, quite literally, in stone, that the teaching of *bel canto* to church choirs was well established in Florence, Italy before the 1430s. The 1431 sculptures by Luca del Robbia in the choir stalls of the Florence cathedral Santa Maria del Fiore, shows the children singing in the mode we know today as the Florentine *bel canto*. Unfortunately, during the Seventeenth and Eighteenth Centuries, a pseudo-*bel canto* raised in Venice and elsewhere, a "Venetian *bel canto*" design for *castrati* not recommended for would-be tenors today. See Nora Hamerman, *op. cit.,* and unpublished research on the Venetian pseudo-*bel canto*.

Rousseauvian degenerate's program-notes). For a serious Classical composition, such as those of Bach, Haydn, Mozart, Beethoven, Schubert, Mendelssohn, Chopin, Schumann, or Brahms, the conveying of musical thought-objects demands:

1. A *bel canto*-singing quality of both vocal and instrumental parts (a pro-vibrato quality).

2. A cleanly executed presentation of the equivalent of the singing-voice's species represented by each passage of a part.

3. Unmuddled polyphonic voice-transparency: no "smashed chords."

4. Execution of each part's required distinctions among the registers and register-passing of each passage's singing-voice equivalence.

5. A clean, beautiful shaping of phrasing, and of execution of individual tones.

6 No camouflaging of a performer's want of musical insight, as by means of today's increasing occurrence of and recklessness in use of manneristically exaggerated tunings, tempi, and rubati.

The relevance of this list of precautions to the subject of musical thought-objects, not a desire to enter into the subtleties of the performer's master class, obliges us to consider here a few, bare minima which illustrate the preconditions of bare polyphonic literacy of performance needed to render an intelligible insight into the composer's musical thought-objects.

Some commonplace abuses of the modern keyboard instrument illustrate most aptly the varieties of antimusical "instrumentalism" fostered even in the practice of numerous known performers. A Classical pianoforte (or, fortepiano) work—such as a keyboard sonata of Mozart, Beethoven, or Schubert—does not know of the existence of chords *per se*; it knows chords only as fleeting shadows of an instrumental parody of *bel canto* vocal polyphony. Each tone of such a chord corresponds to a line of a surrogate for some species of singing-voice vocalization. The performer must bring forth that singing quality, shaping the phrasing and individual tone according to appropriate indications of relative register and register-passing.

An excellent choice of illustration of this point, respecting Classical keyboard compositions, is found in the concluding coda of Beethoven's Opus 111. This is one of Beethoven's major quotations of the Mozart K. 475/457 *Motivführung* derivation from Bach's *Musical Offering*.[62] The pianist should perform this coda in his

---

62. J.S. Bach's *A Musical Offering* consists of two major fugal investigations of the "royal theme"—so named because it was given to him by King Frederick "The Great" of Prussia—along with a number of canonical demonstrations, and a full trio sonata. In the first fugal investigation, the "Three-Part Ricercar" (*ricercar* = research or investigation), Bach presents the theme in the soprano voice:

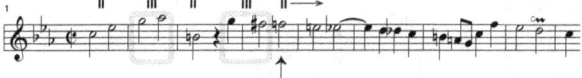

The vocal register indications have been added according to the convention established in *A Manual on Tuning, op. cit.* The third register is indicated by an unfilled box with a thick-shaded outline, the second register is left unmarked, and the first register is denoted either by a filled shaded box (in female voices), or by an unfilled thin-outline box (in male voices).

The theme opens with two notes in the second register, followed by two in the third, and then a steep drop back into the second register on the B natural. The fourth measure then focuses squarely on the III-II register shift by having F♯ on the first, most-emphasized beat, immediately followed by the F natural. The phrase continues downward in the second register, moving by the smallest possible step, the half-step, concluding with a jump to a final cadence.

In contrast to the "Three-Part Ricercar," in the "Six-Part Ricercar" Bach introduces the theme in the *mezzosoprano* voice:

The registration of the theme's first five notes remains similar to that of the soprano; but the registration of the descending figure which follows, shifts attention to the theme's built-in ambiguity between the C-major mode, with its E natural as the third degree of the scale, and C-minor, whose third degree is lowered by a half-step to E natural. This major-minor crossover ambiguity provides the rudimentary thought-object which drives the development of the entire *Musical Offering* series.

The opening measures of Mozart's Sonata for Piano in C-minor, K. 457, demonstrates Mozart's advance in the treatment of the same thematic idea:

(a)

FIGURE 10. *(a)The piano score of the concluding coda of Beethoven's Sonata Op. 111 should be read by the performer not as "instrumental piano music," but as a condensed shorthand version of a string quartet score, which in turn is a reflection of an implied "vocal" score. (b) The same passage has been "exploded" into such a four-part "choral" score, with each voice occupying its own staff. The pianist must always be at pains to observe the implicit register changes as shown in such a "vocal" score. (For an explanation of the boxed register markings, see footnote 62.)*

(b)

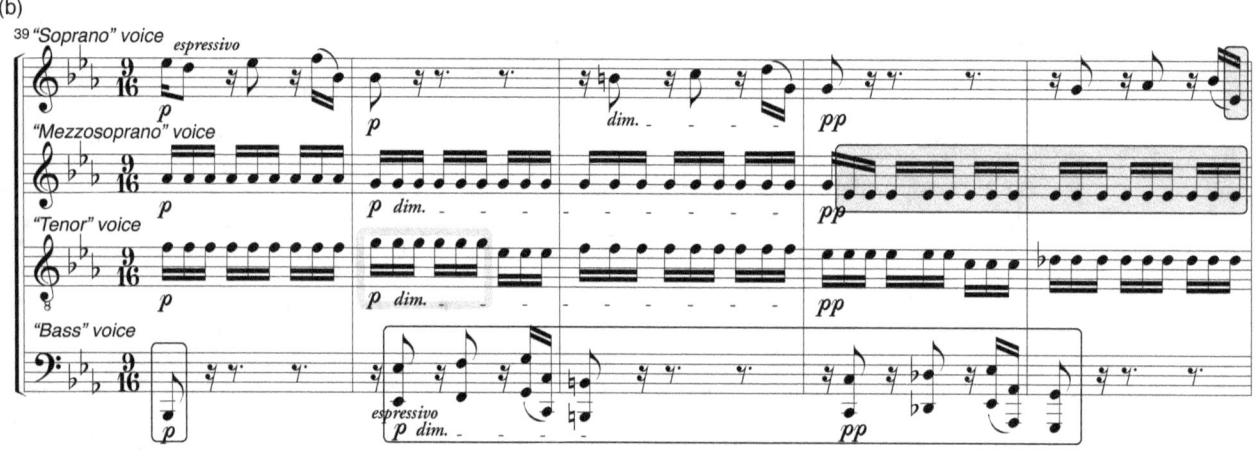

Only the "soprano" and "mezzosoprano" voices in the piano score are shown here. The first five notes are sung in unison by both voices, once again with similar registration. Only in measures 9-13 is the crossover ambiguity presented. The descending mezzosoprano figure is answered by an octave transposition of the same descending figure in the soprano voice.

Mozart subsequently composed his Fantasy in C, K. 475, expressly in order to explicate the principles of his composition of the Sonata K. 457. The opening measures show the ambiguities of the "royal theme" in a most concentrated form:

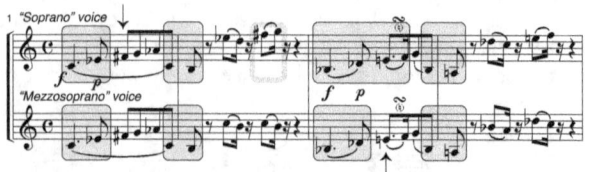

Once again, only the "soprano" and "mezzosoprano" lines of the piano score are shown. The opening unison phrase now presents both the F# and the E natural, which taken together constitute a "limit" beyond which the registrations would cease to be similar. The second measure is dominated by soprano registration, with the high F#. The third and fourth measures, however, are instead dominated by mezzosoprano registration, with its register shift (from below) to the E natural. The poetic shift from the first pair of measures to the second pair is underlined by the phrase markings in measure 3, which differ from those

or her mind as a choral work, and then as a string quartet's parody of that choral performance; then, parody that string quartet's performance at the keyboard. Use the reference to the *bel canto* chorus, to define the properly implied singing-voice species, and with the corresponding registration and register-passing. Then bring these ironies forth from the keyboard, with full contrapuntal transparency (see **Figure 10**).

Next, to the same purpose, let that pianist turn to a related work, the first movement of Chopin's "Funeral March" sonata. This is to be read, of course, as a quotation of Beethoven's Opus 111 (see **Figure 11**). Chopin is a classical composer, not a Lisztian Romantic. His works must be performed with a corresponding polyphonic transparency, without mannerism, not brutishly slaughtered as if in some pagan's human sacrifice, upon the altar of eroticism.

To the same purpose, turn to a selection from Mo-

in the first measure. (Many modern editions of Mozart's piano works have mistakenly altered Mozart's phrase markings to be identical in measures 1 and 3.)

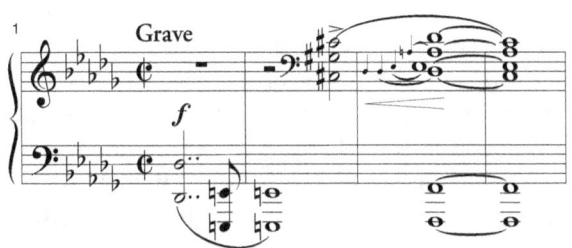

FIGURE 11. *The opening of the first movement of Frederic Chopin's Sonata for Piano in B-flat minor, Op. 35, shown in (a), is a direct quotation from the opening of Beethoven's Sonata Op. 111, shown in (b).*

(a)

zart's post-1781 compositions. Include at least, his 1785/1784 C-minor *Fantasy-Sonata* K. 475/457, and his C-minor 1788/1783 *Adagio and Fugue* K. 546/426. Perform—in the mind, as well—first, the two-keyboard K. 426, performing it as if it were a keyboard echo of a string quartet's parody of a choral work (see **Figure 12**). Next, examine the K. 546 setting for string quartet from this same vantage-point. Apply this same approach to the K. 475 *Fantasy*, up to as far (at least) as the allegro section (see **Figure 13**).

These suggested mental exercises, and analogous ones, must tend to improve that quality of musical insight which borders upon recognition of the relevant thought-objects.[63] To this purpose, it will prove helpful

---

63. In the author's judgment, the relevant musical thought-object is made clear by extended concentration on hearing the performance of the score heard, repeatedly, with experimental variation, in one's imagination.

FIGURE 12. *In December 1783, Mozart composed the Fugue in C (minor) for Two Pianos, K. 426, whose opening is shown in (a). The fact that his reference for the fugue's registration is a string quartet or vocal chorus, is unmistakable from his uncommon use of the vocal tenor clef for the left hand of Piano I, instead of the usual bass clef. The left hand of Piano II opens with the bass voice, while the right hands of Piano I and Piano II enter as mezzosoprano and soprano, respectively. Five years later, in the summer of 1788, Mozart rescored the same fugue for string quartet, adding an adagio introduction and calling it Adagio and Fugue in C (minor),*

to include in such a pedagogical program, emphasis upon post-1781 fugues and fugato composition of Mozart, Beethoven, and Brahms. Bach's work, presented in respect to his pivotal *Musical Offering* and *Art of the Fugue,* should be viewed in the post-1781 context; the post-1781 work by Haydn should then be included.

Once more, bring to bear the crucial point, that the generation of a musical thought-object occurs in essentially the same specific type of way that the appropriate solution is produced for the central paradox of Plato's **Parmenides**: all merely formal, discrete aspects of existence are subsumed by a higher mode of existence, *change.* The relevant, elementary form of this quality of change, is what we have described as "evolutionary negentropy." That point must be applied to define the crucial significance of the Bach fugue for the post-1781 work of Mozart *et al.*

Like a theorem-lattice series, the well-tempered counterpoint of Johann Sebastian Bach, has three prominent features. There is, first, the establishment of great refinement in constructing a formal musical theorem-lattice, the schoolbook side of studies of Bach's fugues, for example. Second, there is the creative development, like that of a science-discovery theorem-lattice, which generates the theories of paradox-resolutions which is the composition as a whole. Third, there is the effort to achieve a higher organic unity of the theorem-lattice series—the unit composition—as a whole, to subsume the *Many* as *One,* as Haydn sought this through his *Motivführung* discovery.

Thus, without all of the leading features of the work of the mature Johann Sebastian Bach, there could not have been Mozart's revolutionary perfecting of Haydn's *Motivführung* discovery. Even as extraordinary a genius as Mozart had become by 1781, could not have produced the six "Haydn" quartets without a regular, extensive working-through of Bach scores which Mozart did, as a participant in the regular Sunday midday salon

(b)

K 546. The corresponding opening measures of the re-scored fugue, shown in (b), show the standard string imitations of the vocal quartet: Violin I (soprano), Violin II (mezzosoprano), Viola (tenor), and Violoncello (bass). Also, Mozart has carefully altered the phrase markings and staccato (lightly accented and separated) markings to suit the particular requirements of the stringed instruments in order better to imitate the choral voices.

FIGURE 13. *Mozart's Fantasy in C, K. 475, especially the sections up to the "allegro" (measures 36ff.), shows the composer's rigorous attention to "choral" registration of this piano work. Measures 15-18 shown here are representative. Compare with Figure 10, which shows Beethoven's direct quotation of these measures.*

of Vienna's Baron Gottfried van Swieten.[64]

There are chiefly two relevant aspects of Bach's perfection of a *bel canto*-premised, strictly well-tempered polyphony (pivoted upon C=256 cycles).[65] There is the formal side of Bach's contrapuntal method, the schoolbook side. There is, otherwise, that higher, creative treatment of lawfully generated contrapuntal anomalies, such as dissonances, a development whose mastery presumes a grounding in the formal, schoolbook side of the matter. On these combined accounts, the Mozart of 1782-1786 stands to the Bach of 1747-1750 as Nicolaus of Cusa of 1440 stood with respect to those manuscripts of ancient Archimedes freshly brought from Greece.

It is strict adherence to properly adduced formalities, which is a precondition for driving any theorem-lattice to beyond its limits, to such an effect that the appropriate, valid paradoxes are generated, and, so, the relevant creative discovery provoked. Thus, the notion of *Motivführung,* like the elementary form of a progressive series of theorem-lattices, presents us with a three-fold picture of the creative process of unified compositional development:

1. Strict rigor respecting the formalities of polyphony, formalities broadly analogous to the consistency of the theorem-lattice.

2. The principle of those singularities which generate a new, higher formalism (e.g., theorem-lattice) out of a paradox generated within the original form. (These two paradoxes are parallel to those of the Plato *Parmenides.*)

3. The *Motivführung* principle, which orders, or im-

plicitly subsumes an ordering of a succession of theorem-lattices as an "evolutionary negentropy" unit of development.

Mozart's work on Bach, especially Bach's discovery represented by the *Musical Offering,* was necessary to generalize the third of these three features of an integrated compositional process. Only a rigorously defined, and ordered, *literate* medium of communication—geometry, music, poetry, or prose—provides the setting wanted to elaborate an anomaly in the needed fashion: to impart that sense of paradox which is associated with the creative-mental processes' successful generation of the relevant thought-object.

There is a second, crucial prerequisite to musical literacy. The lack of any first-rank, living Classical poets, since the generations of Goethe, Schiller, Keats, and Heine, is the cause of the loss—for most educated members of European civilization—or, at least a severe impairment, of the capacity to understand Classical polyphony. Not only is Classical polyphony derived from the *bel canto* vocalization of Classical poetry; the inter-relationships, the continuing interdependence between the two forms, is such that to lose either one is virtually soon to lose the other.

As Friedrich Schiller, Ludwig van Beethoven, and Franz Schubert have emphasized this connection, in their common complaint against Goethe's refusal to tolerate the principles of Classical polyphony,[66] there is this stated essential reciprocity between the two. As Schiller stresses,[67] the composing of a Classical poem begins with an idea of wordless Classical polyphony in the imagination; the subsequent elaboration of this musical image, as poetic vocalization, defines the potential for the germination of the poem. So far as that, Goethe recognized the creation of Classical poetry to occur in

---

64. On Baron Gottfried van Swieten and his salon, see David Shavin, "The battle Mozart won in America's war with Britain," September 6, 1991, *Executive Intelligence Review,*, pp. 22-33. See also Bernhard Paumgartner, ***Mozart,*** München 1991, pp. 299-308.

65. Jonathan Tennenbaum, "The Foundations of Scientific Musical Tuning," ***Fidelio,*** Vol. I, No. 1, Winter 1991.

66. ***Manual,*** Vol. I, ch. 11, *passim.*

67. *Ibid.,* p. 201, notes 2-5.

this manner Schiller so indicated; Goethe's fault was his refusal to grasp the Platonic idea, that something like a *Motivführung* is indispensable to a fully developed Classical musical setting of a poem. Whoever could not follow that argument, with Goethe heading the one faction, and Schiller, Mozart, Beethoven, and Schubert the opposite faction, becomes, as a musician, like that amateur linguist who knows the meanings of none of those foreign-language phrases which he feigns to utter with such fluency.

For reason of such considerations, not only the singer, but the instrumentalist, too, must master this connection between Classical poetry and music, a study usefully pursued through the Italian art-song from Alessandro Scarlatti onward, and continued through that new form of German *Lied* established by Mozart's revolutionary *Das Veilchen*.[68]

As this immediately foregoing argument is illustrated in Volume I of the **Manual on the Rudiments of Tuning and Registration**,[69] the practice of Mozart, Beethoven, Schubert, Schumann, and Brahms (most notably) in composing a *Lied* for a strophic poem[70] is the application of the Haydn-Mozart *Motivführung* principle of composition, as Mozart, chiefly, refined this. This is what Goethe and Reichardt[71] failed to comprehend. This feature of the *Lied*, from Mozart's *Das Veilchen*, through Brahms' *Four Serious Songs*, is also a presentation of the essential characteristics of the *Motivführung* principle, the proper principle of all forms of successful Classical composition, and thus, also, the standard for performance of all such works from that same interval of musical history.

This view of Bach and Classical poetry has an associated benefit not to leave unmentioned here.

The principles of well-tempered polyphony are derived uniquely from those natural characteristics of the human singing voice which are made transparent by *bel canto* training. The setting of the well-tempered scale to values of approximately C=256 and A=430, is not a matter of whim; these values are derived from the biologically-determined spectroscopy of the "chest" of species of human singing voices. The musical system

of well-tempered polyphony is not something externally applied to a poem, to generate a song; Classical poetry is composed, originally, in each case, under the governance of a literally musical idea in the mind of the poet. The vocalization of the poetic line inheres in the idea by which the line itself was originally generated.

Similarly, the definition of a dissonance, and its resolution, are so situated within, and premised upon a natural determination by a well-tempered polyphony. Well-tempered polyphony, at C=256, or A=430, is simply natural beauty, naturally determined. From this, artistic beauty begins, and to this it must return. In this way, Bach's perfection of well-tempered polyphony as a medium of composition provides the rigorous setting for such musical discoveries of higher principles as his own *Musical Offering*, and that for Mozart's revolutionary enhancement of Haydn's *Motivführung* principle.

Yet, that is not sufficient; the principles of well-tempered polyphonic development will not generate great music by themselves. All great composers returned to poetic text, or germs of poetic ideas, not only for their vocal, but also their instrumental works. All Classical musical thematic ideas are derived either from poetry, from original poetic ideas of the musical composer, or from the same type of a wordless idea of vocalization which is the germ of any Classical poem.

Except as we read the work of Mozart, Beethoven, *et al.* in the context both of Bach's development of well-tempered polyphony, and of all true music as an outgrowth of Classical poetry, there could be no genuine musical literacy among professionals or audiences. True musical literacy may be termed "insight," a term which addresses the shadows cast by the essential feature of Classical compositions, "Platonic ideas," otherwise termed "musical thought-objects."

Art Versus 'Materialism'

By means of description and references supplied, we have indicated, above, the nature of the common feature of scientific and artistic creativity. The immediate product of successful activity of this type, is the "thought-object," or *monad* treated here. As we have shown in earlier locations, this individual's creative mental activity is uniquely a *sovereign* experience of, and within the bounds of the individual mind; it is in no way a "collective" social effect.[72] In the case of such a

68. *Ibid.*, pp. 202-208.
69. *Ibid.*, pp. 208-220.
70. See Gustav Jenner, **Johannes Brahms als Mensch, Lehrer und Künstler, Studien und Erlebnisse** (Marburg an der Lahn: N.G. Elwert'sche Verlagsbuchhandlung, G. Braun, 1930). Selected passages appear in *A Manual on Tuning, op. cit.,* chaps. 9-12, *passim.*
71. See *A Manual on Tuning, op. cit.,* chap. 11 *passim.*

72. LaRouche, "Metaphor," *op. cit.,* p. 41; see also "The Science of Christian Economy," in **Christian Economy,** *op. cit.,* pp. 229-240.

valid discovery of a principle of physical science, the created thought-object *subsumes* a definite form of human practice. Immediately, this practice is expressed as an appropriate design of crucial experiment. This experimental (e.g., laboratory) design corresponds to *and subsumes* a consequent principle of machine-tool design. Such machine tools increase mankind's power over nature, *per capita* and per square kilometer. Thus, a "spiritual" act, the creation of such a thought-object, is an efficient causality in the (putatively) "material" domain.[73]

In the composition of Classical polyphony, the result is the same in principle. A problem—a paradox—generated by extended application of ostensibly consistent principles of well-tempered polyphony, provokes a musical thought-object. This process parallels Cusa's discovery of an isoperimetric least action. The generation of the solution, as a thought-object, is played back upon the polyphonic medium. The resolution so effected, is immediately analogous to a design of a crucial experiment. The elaboration of the newly discovered principle of resolution revolutionizes the power of polyphonic composition for entire works.

The point being made here is illustrated most aptly by introducing a contrasting reference to Descartes' *gnostic* dogma, *deus ex machina*.[74]

From the standpoint of mere sense-perception, a paradox in the sensory domain of experimental physics leads to a change in practice, an improvement, in the domain of experimental physics. Similarly, a musical paradox in the domain of tonal sense-perceptions leads to a resolution in the domain of tonal sense-perception. So, Descartes' (largely erroneous) mathematical physics, starts in the material domain and remains there, never departing; so, most formalist musicology situates musical theory. In both cases, the mechanistic, or "materialist" view either denies the existence of a creative process, or insists that cause-and-effect—problem, solution, and result—must all be fully explainable within the domain of sense-perception, never mentioning the creative-mental processes of problem-solving discovery, whether the latter might exist, or not. So, the majority of the most promising candidates for professional careers in physical science are crippled by the *gnostic* dogma, that science—problem, solution, result—must

be explained (or, presumed to be explained) solely by means of "generally accepted classroom mathematics." The same pathological way of thinking, made officially canonical in musicology, has ruined the potential of musicians and audiences alike.

The material, or polyphonic domains, respectively, are each a realm of perception, of sense-perception, and of perceptible features of forms of social practice. Therefore, they are also the domains explicitly referenced by all forms of communication, including algebra and geometry. However, *causality does not occur within the domain of mere perception*; perception is not reality; it is merely the distorted shadow of reality. By "causality," we should not signify "mechanical" or "statistical" correlations; we should signify the cause of those types of change in state which are illustrated by the perceptibly efficient transformation of one theorem-lattice into another, perfectly inconsistent theorem-lattice.

Causality is thus presented to perception paradoxically, as this is presented in Plato's **Parmenides**: as change of this transfinite "dimensionality"; in this way, the efficiency, the reality, the ontological actuality of *change as causality* is presented with crucial undeniability to the faculties of sense-perception (and communication).

This causality, this change, is known to us in association with such various rubrics as "ideas" (Plato), "monads" (Leibniz), "*Geistesmassen*" (Riemann), or this author's "thought-objects." All of these terms reference the same phenomenon, but with slightly different connotations. The difference among them, is that each term was introduced by a different author, each in a unique literary-historical setting. Although all of these terms coincide in significance in the final analysis, their equivalence can be demonstrated only to those individual minds which have experienced all of them, one at a time, each in its own original setting.

For the subject of musical principles, three of these authors suffice. This present author's view of musical thought-objects is cross-referenced principally to the precedent of Platonic aesthetics, and, hence, Platonic ideas. In connection to the Haydn-Mozart revolution of 1781-1786, Friedrich Schiller's definitions of "musical thought-objects" should be included directly.[75]

In scientific and related work, the most profound distinction experienced by the individual, is the distinction between two qualities of mental state. The first

---

73. "On the Subject of Metaphor," *op. cit.,* pp. 36-37.

74. LaRouche, "Metaphor," *op. cit.,* pp. 37-39; see also U.S. Science Policy, op. cit., chap. IV, pp. 108-111 and footnote 3.

75. See *A Manual on Tuning, op. cit.,* ch. 11, *passim.*

state is the application of known, established principles; the second, is the act of discovery of a valid new principle, an act which occurs in the context of solving a true paradox. In music, it is the same; here, the act of discovering an insight into the characteristic idea of the composition's contrapuntal (polyphonic) development, is the creative state of mind.

It is the second of the two kinds of states of mental activity, which corresponds to the experiencing of a relevant thought-object, or thought-objects, as a species of mental life in general. Furthermore, in science and in Classical polyphony, these thought-objects are the cause for which a successful, problem-solving breakthrough to a valid new principle is the manifest consequence.

How is it possible, then, that so many from among even the highest echelons of achievement in modern science and the music profession should object so violently against "Platonic ideas," or be so stubbornly silly as to insist that these "spiritual" existences are not the cause for the new qualities of desired sense-perceptible effects? Since nothing less important than the continuation of human existence could not be achieved but by aid of such continuing scientific and technological progress, how could any self-respecting scientist deny the fact, that such "Platonic ideas" are the cause for manifest scientific progress?

Nonetheless, "Platonic ideas" are ruled out of order, not only by the "Aristotelian gnostic" René Descartes, but by the "materialists" and "empiricists" generally. These foolish denials are not a reflection of innocent sorts of ignorance; they are the influence of that form of modern pagan religion, of modern gnosticism, called the English and French "Enlightenment" of Europe's Seventeenth and Eighteenth Centuries. The anti-Renaissance dogmas of Enlightenment figures such as Rosicrucian Robert Fludd, a co-founder of British Freemasonry,[76] and Descartes, became relatively hegemonic in today's classroom and popular opinion through such enterprises (often, London-backed) as France's Jacobin Freemasonic terror,[77] the 1815 Treaty of Vienna,[78] Lord Palmerston's Mazzinian terrorism of 1848-1849,[79] and Britain's authorship of World War I.[80] All of these, and related developments, were vehicles for efforts to crush out of existence Leibnizian science and to push aside the Classical tradition of Leonardo da Vinci, Raphael, Bach, Mozart, Schiller, and Beethoven in the fine arts.

To understand this aspect of the Enlightenment, two points must be stressed. First, the roots of the Rosicrucian cult in pre-Christian gnostic paganism, and such forerunners of Fludd, Francis Bacon, Descartes, Ashmole, John Locke, *et al.*, as the followers of Mani (Manicheanism) and the Bogomils-Cathars ("Buggers").[81] Second, that the common feature of ancient, medieval, and Rosicrucian gnostics, like Descartes and Immanuel Kant, too, is the emphasis upon denying the efficient, intelligible existence of "Platonic ideas."

Christian civilization defines a secular order in which all persons—all individual human life, is equal under God and natural law, this by virtue of the principle of individual man in *the living image of God (imago viva Dei).*[82] This likeness to the Creator is located in that "divine spark of reason," *creative mental powers,* inhering in each person; thus, is the person in the image of the Creator.[83] Thus, the domain of "Platonic ideas," *monads,* or "thought-objects," is the spiritual realm, while mere sensation and formal media of communication are the putative "material" realm.

The characteristic epistemological feature of all

76. LaRouche, "The Science of Christian Economy," in *Christian Economy, op. cit.,* p. 482.

77. Terror demagogues Danton and Marat were trained and deployed by London, under the immediate supervision of the Earl of Shelburne's (British East India Company's) Jeremy Bentham. The patronage of Robespierre's circles was provided jointly by the London-allied figures Philippe "Egalité," Duke of Orleans, a leading Freemason, and Swiss banker Jacques Necker, who had bankrupted the French monarchy's government. Necker's daughter, the notorious Madame de Staël, a putative friend of Queen Marie Antoinette, conducted the fashionable salon through which the political cause of the Jacobin butchers was greatly assisted.

78. The British government, acting through the Treaty of Vienna's Bourbon Restoration, purged France's leading scientific institution, the Ecole Polytechnique, of its founder, Gaspard Monge and of Monge's brilliantly successful Leibnizian program of education and work. French science collapsed rapidly, then, to the point, that from approximately 1827 on, Germany became the world's leader in science—until Adolf Hitler's time.

79. Lord Palmerston, as Britain's Prime Minister, placed his protégé, Napoleon III, into power in France, as a continuation of Palmerston's earlier deployment of the Mazzinian Freemasonic terror of 1848-49 throughout continental Europe.

80. LaRouche, *U.S. Science Policy, op. cit.,* chap. IV, pp. 103-107.

81. *Ibid.,* chap. IV, pp. 93-97.

82. LaRouche, "The Science of Christian Economy," in *Christian Economy, op. cit.,* pps. 224-236, 301-303, 432-439.

83. Cf. Philo ("Judaeus") of Alexandria, "On the Account of the World's Creation Given by Moses," in *Philo,* Vol. I., trans. by F.H. Colson and G.H. Whitaker, Loeb Classical Libary (Cambridge: Harvard University Press, 1981), §III, pp. 55-57.

gnosticism, is the insistence that the spiritual realm has no desirable form of efficient (causal) interaction with the domain of the ostensibly "material." The gnostic dichotomy divides the universe into two universes, one "spiritual," the other "material," such that the events within each are defined entirely by laws (axioms, postulates) which are "hermetically," inclusively peculiar to the interior of that "half-universe."

So, the anti-Leibniz, neo-Aristotelian, Immanuel Kant, throughout his famous *Critiques,* pronounced *monads* "unknowable," and insisted that there is no principle of truth in the fine arts.[84] Kant's dogma was adopted by the nineteenth-century Romantic adversaries of Schiller and Classical polyphony, as the doctrine of the hermetic separation of *Geisteswissenschaft* (e.g., fine arts) from *Naturwissenschaft* (natural science).[85]

In the history of medieval and modern Europe, every significant spread of gnosticism is always associated with the promotion of Aristotle against Plato.[86] This is associated with a denial of a *Type* of activity[87] distinct as *creative,* and the axiomatic presumption that the internal ordering of the "material" realm is *algebraic* (i.e., mechanical). This Aristotelian, mechanistic view, applied to music, follows the pseudo-scientific tactic of Helmholtz's *Sensations of Tone,* purporting to explain music from the standpoint of a simply mechanistic dogma of percussion and vibrating strings and air.[88]

From medieval times, through the days of Paolo Sarpi,[89] Venice's Padua and Rialto schools, (together with the Isle of Capri of the former pagan Emperor Tiberius), were the center of radiation of the intertwined influences of Aristotle, gnosticism, and usury throughout Western Europe and into the Americas. Out of this influence, there emerged that "Venetian Party" which created British liberalism, and sought to make its captive colony, eighteenth-century Britain, the maritime base for building up a revived pagan Roman world-empire.[90] This "Venetian Party," with its sundry influences upon the continent of Europe, was the employer and sponsor of the gnostic Aristotelianism of Descartes, the seventeenth-century English Rosicrucians, and so on.

Thus, to this day, what we call "European culture," is not an homogenous culture, but rather a yet undecided, continuing war between Christianity, on the one side, and the powerful party of usury, the latter the pagan imperial faction behind the fostering of such gnostic Aristotelianisms as Rosicrucianism, Descartes, empiricism, Immanuel Kant, the nineteenth-century Romantic adversaries of Beethoven and Brahms, and so on.

The power of this gnostic, "Venetian Party" faction, has thus been the means for promoting the hegemony of materialism against both Leibnizian science and Classical fine art. Thus, for reason of that political hegemony of the gnostics in scientific and fine arts institutions, the appreciation of Classical fine art has been crippled. So, in fine arts, as in science, the Manichean dualism of Savigny's Romanticist separation of *Geisteswissenschaft* from *Naturwissenschaft* reigns.[91] So, the musicians learn the language of music, but are denied access to the meaning, the subject-matter of that fine-arts language.

The central issue is thus, that it is the product of creative reason, the musical thought-object, which employs the paradoxical implications of the sensory aspect of the polyphonic language, to impart a recognition of that same musical thought-object in the minds of others. The precious essence of Classical polyphony is in great danger of being lost to the next generations of mankind. The mission adopted by the crafters of the two-volume ***Manual on the Rudiments of Tuning and Registration,*** is to contribute to keeping that imperiled Classical fine-arts knowledge alive for both present and future generations.

84. Immanuel Kant, ***Critique of Judgment,*** *op. cit., passim.* See also LaRouche, "The Science of Christian Economy," in *Christian Economy,* op. cit., pp. 333-334.

85. Berlin University law professor Karl S. Savigny, forerunner of the Nazi legal dogma, was a leading nineteenth-century spokesman for the Romantics' irrationalist dogma toward both art and science. He put into currency today's commonly taught, neo-Kantian dogma asserting an "hermetic" separation of *Geisteswissenschaft* from *Naturwissenschaft.*

86. This began in the Eastern hierarchy of the Church, under the direction of the Byzantine Emperors; there, the banning of Plato, in favor of Aristotle was established many centuries before this gnostic dogma was inserted into Western Europe via Moorish Spain and Venice. Of course, the so-called neo-Platonic cults, which were developed in Byzantium and transported into Western Europe, were actually products of Aristotelianism, not Plato.

87. The term, "*Type,*" is used here in Georg Cantor's sense.

88. Hermann L.F. Helmholtz, **On the Sensations of Tone as a Physiological Basis for the Theory of Music,** 2nd. English edition, trans. by Alexander J. Ellis (New York: Dover Publications, 1954).

89. Paolo Sarpi (1550-1623) was a former Procurator-General of the Servite religious order, who in 1606 was appointed state theologian of Venice on the eve of a bitter fight between Venice and the Catholic Church. He was a leading theoretician of the "new houses" ("*i nuovi*") of the Venetian aristocracy, which took ascendancy against the "old

houses" ("*i vecchi*") in 1582, in one of the most dramatic power struggles in Venetian history.

90. H. Graham Lowry, *How the Nation Was Won: America's Untold Story,* 1630-1754 (Washington, D.C.: Executive Intelligence Review, 1987), pps. 74-76, 158-201.

91. See Andreas Buck, "Das Elend der deutschen Jurisprudenz: Karl von Savigny," **Ibykus,** Vol. III, No. 11, 1984, pp. 47-54.

EDITORIAL

LAROUCHE

Keep Mnuchin Out of Treasury To Avoid a Crash

Jan. 22—After misrepresenting and opposing the Glass-Steagall Act in his confirmation hearings, Steven Mnuchin is a "destructive force" who should be kept out of the Trump Administration Treasury, said economist and *EIR* Founding Editor Lyndon LaRouche today. "He can't be accepted for what he was claiming to be; he's not qualified," LaRouche added, and "he'll make a mess in the Trump Administration. Trump could come out successfully on this [Glass-Steagall] issue; but this guy will mess it up."

As nominee for Treasury Secretary, Mnuchin's exchanges with Sen. Maria Cantwell (D-WA), who has been a lead sponsor of legislation to restore Glass-Steagall, constituted her entire questioning period during the Senate Finance Committee hearing. Despite President Trump having called for "going back to Glass-Steagall" during the campaign, Mnuchin stated his opposition to it. Cantwell pressed the Republican Party platform's call for restoring Glass-Steagall; she also cited official estimates that a huge $14 trillion in economic losses to Americans resulted from the 2007-08 bank blowout, and that Glass-Steagall restoration was necessary to prevent that from happening again now.

"Senator Cantwell's presentation of the case was valid, and it was a case by which she is trying to save this nation," LaRouche said. "We're on the fringe of what could be a terrible collapse."

Mnuchin's response to Cantwell was, "No, I don't support going back to Glass-Steagall as is." He said that he supported the Volcker Rule of the Dodd-Frank Act if modified.

Moreover, Mnuchin made a serious false claim to the Committee, in support of his opposition to Glass-Steagall. He claimed Glass-Steagall, according to a recent Federal Reserve report, "would have very big implication to the liquidity and the capital markets, and banks being able to perform necessary lending." In other words, that Glass-Steagall would result in a less liquid bond market for economic investments, and less lending by banks.

The truth is that this Federal Reserve Report, released this past September, criticized the Volcker Rule on that point, not the Glass-Steagall Act. It is titled, "The Volcker Rule and Market Making in Times of Stress." Its main finding is that "bonds are less liquid during times of stress due to the Volcker Rule." But Mnuchin was distressing the Committee Republicans and large numbers of bankers themselves, by supporting a Volcker Rule.

As to Glass-Steagall and bank credit: FDIC Vice Chairman Thomas Hoenig has repeatedly given expert opinion to Congress and other institutions that during the roughly 60 years when Glass-Steagall was enforced, the United States' capital markets for bank lending and bond issuance were the strongest and deepest in the world.

LaRouche emphasized Jan. 22 that Mnuchin is "doing dirty work which can lead to a deadly collapse in the United States and elsewhere. With what he was pushing, he could cause a crisis which would rapidly bring down the U.S. economy as a whole. We have a new financial system coming about [referring to the international development institutions of China and the BRICS-allied nations]; and here, that begins with restoring Glass-Steagall. So this is international, not only national, in importance."

"I think there is no other option but to state that he must be gotten out" of the Treasury, LaRouche concluded.